CW00689136

Immortal Heroines

Other books by Jacqueline Mehrabi

Discovering the Moon (Leuven: Brilliant Books, 2003)
Discovering the Sun (Leuven: Brilliant Books, 2004)
Jena and Jamie Stories (Skye: Sapling Publications, 1998)
The Love of Bahá'u'lláh (Oxford: One World Publications, 1992)
Mount Carmel: Whatever is Happening? (Leuven: Brilliant Books, 1995)
Nine Holy Days (London: Bahá'í Publishing Trust,1975)
Remember the Rainbow (Oxford: George Ronald, 1985)
Song in the Ground (Oxford: George Ronald, 1985)
Stories of 'Abdu'l-Bahá (London: Bahá'í Publishing Trust, rev. ed. 1995)
Stories for Children (London: Bahá'í Publishing Trust, rev. ed. 1985)
Stories of the Greatest Holy Leaf (London: Bahá'í Publishing Trust, 1997)
Three Gifts of Love (Leuven: Brilliant Books, 2004)

Immortal Heroines

Sarah, Ásíyih, the Virgin Mary, Fátimih, Táhirih, Bahíyyih Khánum

by Jacqueline Mehrabi

. . . the Greatest Holy Leaf [Bahíyyih Khánum] . . .
comparable in rank to those immortal heroines such as
Sarah, Ásíyih, the Virgin Mary, Fátimih and Táhirih,
each of whom has outshone every member of her sex
in previous Dispensations.
Shoghi Effendi

GEORGE RONALD
OXFORD

George Ronald, *Publisher*
Oxford
www.grbooks.com

© Jacqueline Mehrabi 2008
All Rights Reserved

*A catalogue record for this book is available
from the British Library*

ISBN 978–0–85398–528–0

Cover design: Steiner Graphics

Printed in Great Britain
by the MPG Books Group

Dedicated to the memory
of my
daughter Pari
and daughter-in-law Nickie

Contents

The Virgin Mary's Story

Fátimih's Story

Táhirih's Story

Bahíyyih Khánum's Story

Prologue

These stories have been told much as they have come down to us through the centuries. Only occasionally is a possible interpretation given. They contain information from a variety of sources, some of which may be new to the reader. Imagination has been used at times to describe the background to some of the earlier stories but care has been taken not to change the meaning. It is impossible to know if every detail is correct in the older accounts because of the lack of consistent historical records from that time, but still, a surprising amount is known and the heart of each of these stories is true.

These pages are full of miracles, visions and dreams. Sometimes these can be understood literally and they did actually happen. At other times they may have a spiritual significance which needs thinking about. Either way, we can find meaning in them.

Have a wonderful journey into the God-touched lives of these six immortal heroines, who all outshone other members of their sex in the dispensations into which they were born.

Sarah's Story
(c. 2000 BC)
'mother of nations'

In the Desert

It was hot inside the tent. But outside, in the desert, it was even hotter. The sun hurt the eyes and its yellow rays bounced off the burning sand. Even scorpions and snakes knew better than to venture out of their holes in case they fried.

Sarah sighed as she fanned herself in the heat. She was travelling over the parched hills and empty desert with her husband, Abraham, and others who had joined their caravan. Abraham's family was descended from one of Noah's great, great grandsons called Heber and its members were known as Hebrews. As the red sun rose even higher in the sky, Sarah thought of the cool, leafy trees and spacious houses in the town of Ur where she had lived as a child and where she and Abraham had married.

Ur was a town full of riches and life there had been very comfortable. However, although Noah had told people about God several hundred years before, most had forgotten. They still believed in a mythical moon-god from before the time of

1

Noah. The moon-god's wife was believed to be the goddess of the reeds. Their first son was worshipped as the sun-god, their second as the storm-god and their daughter as goddess of the evening star.

Clay idols were made in the images of these gods and goddesses, and people prayed to them for help. Everyone believed that the idols had supernatural powers. Everyone, that is, except for Abraham and Sarah, who knew that these man-made objects didn't have any powers at all. God had spoken to Abraham, telling Him to teach the people again about the one true God who was the creator of everything in earth and heaven.

Sarah had been among the first to believe in Abraham as a Manifestation of God. In fact, she had believed in Him before they were married. But the people of Ur refused to listen to Him, so God told Him to leave. With a few members of the family tribe (including Abraham's father, who still believed in idols and even owned a shop where they were made), Abraham and Sarah had set off across the bleak and empty countryside until they came to a place called Haran.

Abraham's father wanted to stay in Haran. Out of love for the old man, who was still respected as the head of the family, they settled here for many years. When His father died, Abraham felt free to leave. God told Him to travel south to Canaan, promising that the whole of Canaan would belong to His family one day. Sarah often wondered how that would happen – at that moment they didn't even own a small piece of land, let alone a whole country.

They travelled from place to place like nomads. They did have cows, sheep, goats and donkeys, so there was usually milk to make cheese and yoghurt; and on special occasions there was meat, when they could afford to kill one of the animals. But then the rains stopped for months on end and a famine spread throughout the land. The wells became dry and there was no grass to feed the animals. Abraham shared what little food there was among everyone. Sarah did what she could for the women and children who came to her tent for help but there was nothing she could do about the weather.

Abraham waited for God to tell Him what to do next but this time no message came. In the end, He decided that the family's only hope was to keep moving until they reached the land of Egypt and the lush green fields by the River Nile.

The Big Idol

As they travelled, Sarah remembered how, before they had left their home in Ur, Abraham had tried every way He could to persuade His father and the rest of the community not to worship idols.

'What are these images that you love so much?' He asked them one day.

'They are the gods whom our fathers worshipped,' they replied.

'But there is only one God, not many,' Abraham told them. 'And He is greater than anything we can ever understand. He is the Lord of the heavens and the earth.'

They were not convinced, so Abraham said He would prove it to them.

As soon as they left the temple, Abraham took an axe and broke all the clay idols except for the biggest one. He then hung the axe round the neck of the big idol. When the people returned, they angrily demanded to know who had destroyed the idols. To help them understand that the idols had no power to do anything, let alone create the heavens and the earth, Abraham pretended that the big idol had broken the rest. They didn't believe Him, of course, because, deep down, they knew this was impossible.

'Then ask the idols themselves who has broken them,' said Abraham.

'But you know they cannot speak!' the people replied, feeling bewildered.

'Then tell them to make themselves whole again!' said Abraham.

'They can't do that either,' wailed the people.

'Then why do you worship them?' asked Abraham. 'If they can't do anything, how can they help you? Why don't you worship the one true God instead of useless clay objects that you have made yourselves?'

Even though Abraham had proved His point, the priests and the king of the land continued to be angry with Him because He refused to worship the idols as they did. Sarah remembered how worried she had been when they decided to give Abraham a test to decide whether or not He was telling the truth. The test was for Him to walk through a fire without being burnt. If He came through the fire unhurt, they said that would mean He was telling the truth. However, if He were burnt, then that would mean he was telling a lie and they would continue to believe in their idols.

The story says that Abraham bravely walked through the fire and God protected him from being harmed. The king and the priests, however, went back on their word and still refused to believe Him. The fact is, they didn't want to change their old ways. It was then that God told Abraham to leave Ur and to find people who wanted to listen to the truth.

Pharaoh's Gift

Sarah was very beautiful, and people wrote poems and songs and stories about her. But there was one thing that made both Abraham and Sarah sad: they did not have any children. However, Abraham was not too worried because God had told Him that one day He would have as many descendants as there were stars in the sky.

God had also said of Sarah, 'I will bless her, and moreover I will give you a son by her. I will bless her, and she shall give rise to nations.'

When the family finally arrived in Egypt, Pharaoh heard about this lovely woman called Sarah who had just arrived in his country. He ordered his guards to bring her to his palace, and when he set eyes on her, he was bedazzled by her looks and wanted to marry her. At first, he thought she was Abraham's sister and, indeed, she was related to Him, but when he discovered she was actually Abraham's wife, he became angry and disappointed and knew he had to let her go.

When Sarah left the palace, Pharaoh gave her the gift of one of his slaves – a young handmaid called Hagar.

Birth of Ishmael

Time passed, and Sarah became too old to have a baby, but she and Abraham longed for a son. Abraham had even thought of adopting His servant boy, Eliezer, and making him His heir, even though Eliezer was not related to Him in any way. Then Sarah remembered that God had said that Abraham's descendants would be so many it would be impossible to count them and that one day they would form a mighty nation. How could that happen if Abraham did not have any children of His own? After deep thought she came to a decision. It had to do with her handmaid, Hagar.

Although Hagar was a servant, she was treated like a member of the family. Sarah told her about God and they became good friends. Sarah would have been content with life except for the problem of being too old to give Abraham a son. But, she thought to herself, Hagar wasn't too old, and it was the custom of the time for men to have more than one wife, so there was no reason why Abraham shouldn't have another. In fact, it would have been expected. So Sarah suggested to Abraham that Hagar should become His second wife. This seemed to be an excellent solution to the problem and Abraham agreed.

It was understood that as Sarah was the first wife, she would raise Hagar's children as her own. This also was a common practice at the time. However, Hagar was young and not very wise and when she became pregnant she thought she should now be the head wife instead of Sarah. Things were not working out as well as Sarah had expected, and she and Hagar began to quarrel. One day Hagar left the house and ran away into the desert. God heard her crying and an angel appeared to her, telling her to return to Abraham and Sarah. The angel also told her that she would have a son named Ishmael who would be the head of many tribes one day. So Hagar went back.

The day came when a son was born to Hagar. He was named Ishmael, which means 'God hears'.

Sarah was pleased about the birth of Hagar's baby but she still longed to have a child of her own.

Birth of Isaac

Thirteen more years passed and one day, as Sarah was in her tent and Abraham was sitting outside His, something mysterious happened. Three men appeared, apparently from nowhere. Abraham bowed to the ground at their feet. He knew they were some kind of heavenly angels sent to Him with a message from God.

The most important one asked, 'Where is your wife, Sarah?'

'There, in the tent,' replied Abraham, pointing to Sarah's tent.

The angel said, 'I will return this time next year and Sarah your wife will have a son.'

Now Sarah was listening to everything that was being said and when she heard she would have a baby, she laughed out loud because she knew she was now far too old to have a child.

The angel heard her and said, 'Why did Sarah laugh and say, "Will I really have a child, now that I am old?" Is anything too hard for the Lord? I will return to you at the appointed time next year and Sarah will have a son.'

It happened just as the angel had promised. Exactly one year later, Sarah gave birth to a little boy. He was a lovely baby and Sarah was overjoyed.

'God has brought me laughter,' she said, 'and everyone who hears about this will laugh with me.'

God told Abraham to call the baby Isaac, which means 'he laughs'.

Sarah was now happy, but the birth of little Isaac did not make the situation between herself and Hagar any better. Hagar was worried that Abraham would love Sarah's son more than He loved hers and would choose Isaac as His heir instead of Ishmael. And Sarah was worried because young Ishmael often mocked his baby half-brother.

Abraham did not know what to do, for he loved both his sons. In the end it was decided that Hagar and Ishmael should live somewhere else so that peace could return to the family.

God told Abraham not to worry because He had blessed both His sons and their descendants.

A Holy Cave

Abraham and Sarah had another 40 happy years together before Sarah died.

Abraham wanted to bury her in a special place, somewhere that would honour her memory. He had long known of a cave which was thought to be holy. It was said that Adam had chosen to be buried there but so deep inside it was impossible for anyone to find Him. Perhaps that was just a story but for hundreds of years people had gone there to pray; and when Abraham saw a vision of Adam and Eve in the cave surrounded with flowers, He decided this was where He wished His beloved Sarah to be buried.

At first the owner did not want to sell his valuable property, but eventually he agreed. The cave and a field next to it were the very first plots of land Abraham owned in Canaan.

Abraham was highly respected as a wise and wealthy leader in the region, and kings and important people for miles around came to Sarah's funeral. She was lovingly laid in the holy cave and for seven days everyone mourned, and all the inhabitants of the land came to comfort Abraham and Isaac.

Isaac and Rebecca

Isaac missed his mother so much he could not be comforted. Three years passed and his heart was still heavy with grief. His father wondered what to do to help him and decided it would a good idea if His son were to marry.

Abraham called Eliezer to Him.

'I am weak with old age,' He told His faithful servant. 'I do not know when I will die. I want you to go on my behalf to the land of Haran to fetch a wife for my son Isaac.'

And he sent Eliezer off with ten men mounted on ten camels laden with jewels.

When he reached the outskirts of Haran, Eliezer wondered how he was going to find the right wife for Isaac. He stopped near a well and began to pray, asking God to help him. As he prayed, an idea came into his head: he would ask one of the women collecting water from the well to give him a drink. If she agreed and also offered to give water to his camels, he would take this as a sign from God that she was the one who would make a good and loving wife for Isaac.

Even before he had finished his prayer, a beautiful girl passed by with a water jar on her shoulder.

'Please give me a drink,' Eliezer called out to her.

The girl lowered her jar and said, 'Drink, and I will water your camels as well.'

She poured the rest of the water into a trough for the camels and then returned to the well many times to refill her jar until all the camels had been thoroughly watered.

Eliezer felt confident that she would be a wonderful wife for Isaac and he gave her two gold bracelets and a gold ring in appreciation of her kindness. There was just one question he needed to ask before he could be absolutely sure: Abraham had said that Isaac's future wife should come from a branch of His own family, so Eliezer asked:

'Whose daughter are you?'

When the girl told him the name of her mother and said that she was the daughter of the King of Haran, Eliezer realized she was related to Abraham through her grandfather. He also learned that her name was Rebecca.

When Eliezer met the family and gave them the gold and jewels he had brought as a gift from Abraham, they agreed to the marriage but suggested that he should return home and Rebecca would follow some time later.

'I cannot return to my master without her!' protested Eliezer, feeling worried that the family would keep both Rebecca and the gold! Abraham had told him to bring back a bride for Isaac and, with God's help, that is what he intended to do.

It was decided to ask Rebecca what she thought. When she was asked if she wished to return with Eliezer or wait until a later date, she said she would like to leave with him.

When Eliezer returned home with Rebecca there was much rejoicing. Isaac was delighted with his bride. Abraham was also pleased and gave Rebecca the tent that had once belonged to Sarah. Sarah had always welcomed the poor and ill to her tent, and Abraham was happy that once again its doors would be open to all who needed help.

The Children of Abraham

The time came when Abraham also died and hundreds came to His funeral. Among them was Ishmael. It was the first time he had returned home, although His father had visited him over the years and they had worked together building a shrine on a holy site associated with Adam.

By coming to the funeral, Ishmael made his peace with Isaac and the two brothers buried their father in the cave with Sarah.

The grandchildren of Isaac and Rebecca formed the twelve tribes of Israel. As for Ishmael, he married a girl from Egypt and founded a great family which became the Arab race.

After the death of Sarah, Abraham married His third wife, Katurah, and had six more sons and probably several daughters. Abraham's descendants spread far and wide and many did great things, just as God had promised. Like Abraham, some of them also became Manifestations of God.

❧

So this is Sarah's story. Although she lived over four thousand years ago, she is remembered as being the most important woman to have lived at that time in history. She had many tests and difficulties in her long life, but her faith was very strong and she taught all the women around her about the oneness of God. While Abraham is remembered as 'the Father of Nations', Sarah is remembered as their mother.

Ásíyih's Story
(c. 1500 BC)
'the tender heart'

The Secret

Miriam was ten years old when her mother told her that she would soon have a baby brother or sister. But although her mother sounded pleased, Miriam noticed that she looked worried.

'Are you not happy, Mother?' she asked.

Her mother sighed. How could she be happy? Along with thousands of other Hebrews, they were slaves of a tyrant king, the Pharaoh of Egypt, and she feared for her baby's life.

The particular tribe the family belonged to was called the Levites, after one of Abraham's great-grandsons named Levi. Miriam's mother was one of Levi's daughters. The men of the tribe were usually priests, as were some of the women, but that wasn't saving them now they were slaves in Egypt.

'Let us hope this baby is a girl,' said Miriam's mother, smiling at her daughter and her three year old son, Aaron.

Miriam knew what her mother meant, and her heart missed a beat. She knew that the proud and idol-worshipping Pharaoh believed that one greater than himself was about to be born and had ordered two midwives to secretly kill every Hebrew baby boy they delivered.

The midwives had no intention of carrying out this cruel order, and when Pharaoh demanded to know why they hadn't obeyed him, they made excuses, saying that Hebrew women were so strong and healthy the babies were already born by the time they arrived, so it had been impossible to secretly kill them! In the end, Pharaoh became impatient and ordered his soldiers to kill the babies instead.

'Drown them in the River Nile,' he ordered. 'Not one must be left alive.'

Everyone was afraid, and Miriam's father told her mother to keep indoors as much as possible so no one would know she was pregnant.

'Be careful, Yocheved,' he told her tenderly. 'Send Miriam on your errands so no one sees you.'

At night, when Miriam and her brother Aaron were lying on the mat that formed their bed in the corner of the tent, they could hear their mother and father praying that God would protect the baby when it was born.

Then, one morning, Miriam woke up to the sound of a baby crying. She looked across at her mother, who whispered, 'Don't tell anyone, but you have another little brother!'

Palaces and Pyramids

'It seems so cruel,' protested Queen Ásíyih, who was the wife of Pharaoh, King of Egypt. She was distressed at the thought of babies being killed, especially as she and her husband had no children of their own and she longed to hold a baby in her arms. Tears filled her eyes as she begged her husband to change his mind.

Pharaoh looked fondly at his lovely wife, but he didn't bother to reply. Women always had tender hearts, he thought to himself as he adjusted his two crowns, one fixed on top of the other, which he wore on his head.

Ásíyih knew her husband thought himself more important than any other king. He believed he was some sort of god who should be worshipped and obeyed. People bowed low when he rode among them, and his Egyptian subjects prayed to him as though he were God Himself. Thousands of his subjects, as well as the Hebrew slaves and their children, spent their entire lives working from dawn to dusk to build his palaces and that huge pointed tomb of his rising out of the desert.

The tomb was shaped like a pyramid and was a palace for Pharaoh to live in when he died. Its point represented the sun shedding its rays upon the earth. That's how Pharaoh thought of himself – as a sun-god giving life to the world. When he died, he would be sealed inside the pyramid and from there he believed he would rise up to heaven and rule forever. To help him on his journey from this world to the next, there would be a boat inside the pyramid, piles of food and slaves who would be buried alive with him when he died. Ásíyih knew she would probably be buried with him too. She had never seen inside but she had heard it had miles of gold-lined passages and halls hung with jewels.

Life in the palace was the only kind Queen Ásíyih had ever known. But lately she had begun to worry about the cruel way the slaves were being treated. In the fields beyond the palace, hard taskmasters could be seen beating those who collapsed from tiredness. Some of the slaves were just small children, three or four years old, and they looked very thin. One of their jobs was to run around the fields where wheat was being sown and wave their arms to frighten away any birds who tried to eat the seed. If a bird did manage to land and eat some of the seed, the children would be beaten within an inch of their lives. Many of the slaves died when they were young.

If Pharaoh ever guessed that his wife seriously doubted his orders to kill the babies, Ásíyih knew she could be killed as well. In a way, she felt like a prisoner, although she was surrounded with gold and beautiful things and never had to do any work.

The Rush Basket

Miriam was with her family eating a meal of barley bread and bean stew. Her mother was nursing the baby, who was now three months old.

'We can't keep Him a secret much longer,' said Yocheved, stroking her baby's plump cheeks and giving a smile when He chuckled. 'Someone will be sure to report us and then the soldiers will come and kill Him.'

Miriam lost her appetite and shuddered as she imagined having to hand her baby brother over to the soldiers. She pushed away her plate and looked anxiously at her mother and father.

'But God has told me what to do,' said Yocheved. 'When the baby was born, God told me to feed Him for as long as possible, and then, when it became too dangerous to keep Him at home any longer, to put Him in the river.'

Miriam stared in horror at her mother. 'But He will die!' she exclaimed.

'No, Miriam,' her mother consoled her. 'God said I should not be frightened or worried and that the baby would somehow be brought back to me.'

She smiled reassuringly at her daughter. God had told her something else as well, but she decided it would be safer not to tell Miriam about it yet, just in case she mentioned it to someone and it put the baby in even greater danger. God had told her that one day people would know that her baby son was a Manifestation of God. Pharaoh had been right when he suspected that one greater than himself was about to be born.

Yocheved turned to her husband.

'Amram, I am going to make a strong basket out of rushes,' she told him. 'And then I will line it with clay and tar to make it waterproof so it will float.'

Miriam ran outside to collect pieces of wool left on thorn bushes by passing sheep so her mother could make a soft mattress for the baby to lie on. Last of all, her mother covered her little boy with a soft blanket.

'This is a little ark to keep you safe,' she whispered as she kissed Him.

She beckoned Miriam to follow her outside. They went to the river and Yocheved carefully put the basket into the water. She gave it a gentle push and it floated down the river, round the bend and out of sight.

'Run after it!' Yocheved told her daughter. 'But stay hidden! Don't let anyone see you! Then come back and tell me what happens.'

The Queen and the Baby

One of the palace servants was walking by the river when he heard the sound of crying. Parting the reeds at the river's edge, he was surprised to find a baby in a basket. He gently picked Him up and took Him to Queen Ásíyih.

Ásíyih's heart melted when she saw the baby and she loved Him at once. But when her husband was told, he said the little boy should be killed immediately.

'Let us adopt Him,' begged Ásíyih. 'If we bring Him up in the palace, He will never know he was once a slave. He will be one of us.' She thought desperately of something that would persuade her husband to change his mind and added, 'He might become useful later in our fight against the Israelites!' (the Israelites being another name for the Hebrews).

Pharaoh hesitated. Perhaps Ásíyih was right and the boy would prove useful to them when He grew up. To her delight, he said she could keep Him. But at first she couldn't stop the baby crying. He was missing His mother, and although He was hungry, He continued to cry when nurses tried to feed Him.

Miriam had followed the servant when he had taken her little brother to Queen Ásíyih and nobody had taken any notice of her in all the excitement over the baby. Now she made her way into the presence of the queen.

'Your Majesty, I know of a slave woman who has just lost her baby and could breastfeed this baby for you,' she said, bowing low to the ground.

Queen Ásíyih told her to fetch the woman, and Miriam ran back along the river bank to tell her mother that she was needed at the palace.

Life in the Palace

Ásíyih named the baby Moses, and nobody guessed that the nurse who looked after Him and fed Him was really His mother!

Ásíyih and Pharaoh loved their adopted son and He was treated like a prince. However, one day, when Moses was about one year old, something happened that nearly changed everything. A story is told how the baby was sitting on Pharaoh's knee when He reached up, and taking the crown from Pharaoh's head, put it on His own. There was a gasp of horror from everyone in the hall. The court magicians thought this was a very bad sign. Was the child wishing to be greater than Pharaoh? They demanded that He be tested.

Two metal boxes were brought. One was filled with gold. The other was filled with hot coals. If the baby took the gold, then the magicians said it would mean He wished to be greater than Pharaoh and should be killed. If He took a piece of coal, then it would be all right.

Everyone watched to see what little Moses would do. It is said that He reached out a hand and took a piece of hot coal. Then, as babies tend to do, He put the coal into His mouth. Ásíyih sighed in relief. Her baby's life was spared. He did develop a stutter, though, which He had throughout His life, and some people say it was because of the hot coal that had burnt His mouth when He was a baby.

Pharaoh's Threats

Ásíyih watched over her adopted child and loved Him more every day. As He grew older and became a young man, He told her about the one true God and said she should stop worshipping the gold idols in the temples. Ásíyih listened and believed what Moses said. But when Pharaoh heard that his wife was worshipping God more than she worshipped him, he was furious. And when Moses performed a miracle in front of the court magicians and they all bowed down and said they believed in God too, Pharaoh threatened to punish them all.

'Believe ye in Him before I give you permission?' he shouted. 'Surely this must be your leader, who has taught you magic! Be sure I will cut off your hands and feet on opposite sides, and I will have you crucified on trunks of palm-trees: so shall ye know for certain which of us can give the more severe and the more lasting punishment!'

Ásíyih prayed to God: 'My Lord, build for me a house with Thee in heaven, and save me from Pharaoh and his works, and save me from the unjust people.'

And she ran away from her cruel husband.

Moses Frees the Slaves

One day Moses saw a slave being savagely beaten by an Egyptian soldier and He ran to defend him. Moses was so angry He killed the soldier. But although He had saved the life of the slave, His own life was now in great danger. He knew that when Pharaoh heard what had happened, he would order the soldiers to kill Him. He had to flee from Egypt and live in another land, where

He became a shepherd and later married.

As He was looking after His sheep one day, He saw a fire burning on the top of a mountain. When He went closer, He heard the mighty voice of God coming out of the flames, commanding Him to return to Egypt and tell Pharaoh to set the slaves free.

Moses obeyed and returned to Egypt, although He did not know what fate awaited Him. Queen Ásíyih was no longer alive. The old Pharaoh had also died but the new one was just as proud and cruel.

When Moses went to the palace and told Pharaoh what God had said, Pharaoh refused to release the slaves. Instead, he shouted, 'I care nothing for the Lord: and I tell you I will not let the slaves go!' And he began to treat them even more cruelly than before.

Then disaster after disaster afflicted Pharaoh's kingdom: the river turned to blood and all the fish died; there was a plague of frogs; lice crawled over every man, woman and animal; a cloud of insects attacked everyone; an illness spread among the cows and sheep; people became covered in boils; huge hail stones and fire struck the land; locusts filled the sky and ate every leaf in sight; darkness covered the land for three days; and, finally, the worse thing of all, every firstborn Egyptian child died, including Pharaoh's son.

Up until then, Pharaoh had stubbornly refused to give in, even though Moses told him that it was God who was sending these terrible plagues and they wouldn't stop until the slaves were freed. But when Pharaoh's own son died, he gave in and said that all the slaves were free to leave.

Thousands followed Moses out of the country, including His

sister, Miriam, and His brother, Aaron. But Pharaoh broke his promise and sent his soldiers after them, and they were nearly caught as they crossed the Red Sea.

It was a miracle that saved them. As the slaves came to the sea, there was a mighty roar as the water parted, leaving a dry path on the seabed all the way across to the other side. Moses and His followers began to run along the path to safety but Pharaoh's army came thundering along on horseback behind them, getting closer and closer.

The fleeing slaves were nearly caught, but just as they reached the safety of the opposite bank, the water closed in behind them, drowning all of Pharaoh's army. Some people say that this extraordinary event may have been caused by an earthquake under the sea, which could have made the water part for several minutes. But, however it happened, it was still a miracle that it occurred exactly at that moment.

For the last four hundred years the descendants of Abraham had been treated as slaves and now, at last, they were free. After a further 40 years of wandering through deserts and lonely places, they finally settled in a land of their own called Canaan. God had promised Abraham that this land would one day belong to His descendants and that promise had now come true.

Moses died two years before they reached the Promised Land, but during the journey God gave Him wonderful teachings to help people lead good and happy lives. Some of these teachings are called the Ten Commandments. They tell us how important it is to love and obey God and our parents, and that we should not kill, or lie, or do anything that would make others unhappy.

We don't know many details about the life of Ásíyih but we do know that she had a tender heart and was a loving mother to her adopted son, Moses. If it hadn't been for her love, Moses would have been thrown back into the river to die. We also know that she had a strong faith and was extraordinarily brave when her husband threatened to do terrible things to her. One account says that she ran away from him while another says that, in the end, he killed her because she believed in God.

The Virgin Mary's Story
(c. 15 BC – 50 AD)

'blessed among women'

A Gift from God

From the very beginning Anna knew there was something special about her baby. She had prayed to God to give her a child in her old age, just as, two thousand years before, He had given Abraham's wife Sarah a child when she was old. As Anna prayed, an angel had appeared to her, saying, 'Anna, Anna, the Lord has heard your prayer. You shall conceive and bear a child, and your offspring shall be spoken of in the whole world.'

Anna's heart had overflowed with happiness at this news. She had turned her face to God and said, 'O my Lord! I dedicate unto Thee what is in my womb for Thy special service. Accept this from me, for Thou hearest and knowest all things.'

At about the same time, an angel had also appeared in a vision to Anna's husband, Yoachim, as he was walking with his sheep over the hills outside Jerusalem. When the angel told him the joyful news that he and his wife would at last have a child, Yoachim was as delighted as Anna, for they had long given up all hope of having children.

In due course the baby was born. But, at first, Anna was disappointed, for the baby was a girl and she had hoped for a boy who would grow up to be a religious scholar or an important leader able to perform a great service in the path of God. It was almost impossible at the time for a girl to have the opportunity to achieve greatness in this way. However, God had a divine plan for the baby girl, and He said to Anna: 'I have named her Mary (Maidservant of God) and I give her and her descendants to your protection.'

Childhood

On Mary's first birthday her father prepared a grand feast for her and invited the chief priests and elders and holy ones from the Temple. Then, when she was three, her parents decided to take her to the Temple in Jerusalem to be looked after and educated by the high priest, whose name was Zacharias. Mary's parents knew their daughter was a gift from God and they wanted to make sure she would be guided to lead a good and holy life, just as God had commanded them. It was a happy arrangement, as the priest was married to Anna's cousin Elizabeth and the two families knew each other well.

When three-year-old Mary was first taken to the Temple, it is said she danced with joy on the altar and everybody loved her.

For the next nine years she was educated in the Temple and when she was 12 it was decided it was time for her to become engaged to be married.

The Engagement

Mary's parents had probably died by this time, for they were already old when she was born, so it fell to Zacharias to arrange everything for the engagement. He had a vision from God telling him to invite 12 widowers of good character to the Temple. Each was told to bring a hollow rod with him so that a lottery could be held to decide who should marry Mary.

Zacharias gathered all the rods from the men and took them with him when he went into the Temple to pray. When he came out, he examined the rods to see if any special sign had appeared on them during the prayers, but none had, so he returned them to the men. As he handed the last rod to the last man, a dove flew out of it and landed on the man's head. The priest took this as a sign from God that this was the man who should become Mary's husband.

When Mary asked the name of the man she was now engaged to, she was told it was Joseph. He was known to be a good carpenter and a good man. She also learned that Joseph could trace his ancestors hundreds of years back to a great king called David, who was descended from Abraham and Sarah.

Before the actual marriage took place, Mary and Joseph were engaged for several years and it was during this time that a miracle happened.

Messages from Angels

Mary was by herself, drawing water from a well, when she heard a voice say:

O Mary! Blessed art thou among women.

Mary looked around but there was no one there. She began trembling so much she had to sit down. Then she saw a vision of an angel standing before her. He told her not to be frightened as he was only a messenger from God come to tell her she would have the gift of a pure little boy.

'Fear not, Mary, for thou hast found favour with God,' he told her. 'And, behold, thou shalt conceive in thy womb, and bring forth a son, and shalt call His name Jesus.'

Mary was both confused and excited. First, she ran to the Temple to tell Zacharias what had happened, and he said she would be blessed among all the generations of the world. Then she went to the house of Elizabeth, who was Zacharias's wife and her mother's cousin and was also pregnant.

When Mary told Elizabeth what the angel had said, Elizabeth felt her own baby leap for joy in her womb.

But Mary began to think that she was not good enough for such a holy blessing. She was also worried because Joseph had been away working for many months building houses near the Sea of Galilee, and they were still only engaged and not yet married. What would he say when he knew she was pregnant? How could she explain about the angel telling her that she had been chosen to have a holy child? She knew she had not done anything wrong but she was sure Joseph wouldn't believe her.

Mary stayed for three months with Elizabeth, and then she went home and hid so that no one would see she was pregnant. But after another three months had passed, Joseph returned, and when he saw Mary was expecting a baby he was very upset.

As well as being disappointed in her, he felt he had failed to protect her.

'Why have you done this and forgotten God?' he asked in bewilderment.

Mary cried bitterly and said, 'I am pure, and have not been with a man. As the Lord my God lives, I do not know how I am with child!'

Joseph did not want to bring public shame on Mary, so he decided that he would say nothing about her being pregnant but would quietly break off his engagement to her and that would be the end of the matter. However, before he had the chance to do this, an angel spoke to him in a dream, saying: 'Joseph, son of David, do not be afraid to take Mary home with you as your wife. It is by the Holy Spirit that she has conceived this child. She will bear a son; and you shall give Him the name Jesus, for He will save His people from their sins.'

Joseph did as the angel said, although he was still upset and did not understand how such a thing could have happened.

Jesus is Born

Augustus Caesar was emperor of the Roman world at the time and he wanted to know how many people were living in his empire, so he ordered everyone to return to the towns and villages where they had been born in order to register their names. Joseph and Mary had to travel from the town of Nazareth to Bethlehem to be registered, as Bethlehem was where Joseph's family had originally come from. Joseph's sons from his first marriage went with them.

Mary was nearly nine months pregnant, and as they came

near the end of their journey she felt the first pangs of childbirth and had to stop beneath a palm tree in the desert to rest. She was hungry and thirsty and knew she could not go on any longer. As she leant against the trunk of the tree, she heard a voice say, 'Grieve not, for your Lord has provided a river beneath you, and if you shake the trunk of the tree, fresh ripe dates will fall for you to eat.'

As Mary ate the sweet dates from the tree and drank the clear water from the river, Joseph looked for a suitable place for the baby to be born. But all around them was rock and desert, and further on, in the town of Bethlehem, all the inns were full because of the large number of people coming to register their names for the census.

One story says that Mary's baby was born in the stable of one of these inns. Another says that Joseph took her to a nearby cave and left her in the care of his sons while he went to find a midwife. But wherever it happened, the baby was safely born and He was a beautiful little boy.

When He was eight days old, the baby was circumcised, as was the custom for Jewish baby boys, and He was given the name of Jesus.

Signs and Dangers

Many strange and wondrous things happened around the time baby Jesus was born. That very night some shepherds who were looking after their sheep on the hills outside Bethlehem could hardly believe their eyes when they saw a vision of an angel accompanied by a multitude of other holy beings. The shepherds were terrified at first, especially when they found themselves surrounded by a heavenly light, but the angel told them not to be afraid as a Great One from God had just been born.

Then holy men who lived in a neighbouring land to the east were guided by a star to Jerusalem, which is close to Bethlehem. They were followers of the Prophet Zoroaster and had discovered through studying the stars and the prophecies in their holy writings that another great Prophet had been born. When they arrived in Jerusalem they told people that they had come to worship a newborn child who would be King of the Jews.

When King Herod the Great heard this he was not pleased. After all, he was the king of the land, so what was this talk of another king? He privately met with the wise men and pretended he wanted to honour this remarkable child.

'Go, and make a careful inquiry about the child,' he told them. 'When you have found Him, report to me, so that I may go myself and pay Him homage.'

Of course, he had no intention of doing any such thing; when the child was found, he intended to have Him killed.

The wise men continued to follow the star, which led them to Bethlehem. There they found Jesus with His mother and they bowed down before them and gave gifts to the baby. But they were warned in a dream not to tell King Herod where Jesus was because the king wanted to kill Him, so when it was time for them to leave, they secretly returned to their own country by a different route without going back through Jerusalem.

That same night, as Joseph was sleeping, an angel appeared to him in a dream telling him to immediately take Mary and her baby and escape to Egypt.

'Stay there until I tell you,' said the angel, 'for Herod is going to search for the child to do away with Him.'

Joseph woke up in alarm, and while it was still dark, he and Mary took the baby and fled over the border to Egypt.

Later, when King Herod learned how he had been tricked by the wise men, who had left the country without first reporting to him, he became very angry. He thought the special child would still be in Bethlehem; so, just as the Pharaoh had done over a thousand years before when Moses had been born, he ordered all baby boys in the area who were two years old or under to be killed.

But by this time, Mary, Joseph and the baby were many miles away, and they stayed in hiding until it was safe for them to return home.

Visiting the Temple

When Jesus was one year old, Mary took Him to the Temple to be blessed; and something unusual happened there which filled her with wonder. An old man called Simeon came up to them, took Jesus in his arms and prophesied His future greatness and glory. Simeon said that Jesus would suffer in the future because people would not believe the divine message He would tell them. Simeon also told Mary, 'And you too shall be pierced to the heart.' Mary did not understand exactly what he meant, but she treasured his words and remembered them.

Back home in Nazareth, as soon as He was old enough, Jesus had to help His father in his carpentry shop, for the family was poor. But each year they all returned to Jerusalem for a festival called Passover, and when Jesus was 12 years old they made the journey as usual.

Everyone who was able to do so travelled to Jerusalem for Passover. The Passover festival celebrated the time when God had told Moses to rescue the Israelites from slavery and He had led them safely out of Egypt. There was always much rejoicing when the people got together and remembered this part of their history.

As usual, the celebrations lasted for several days, and when they were over, Mary and Joseph, together with a crowd of their friends and relations who were travelling with them, set off to return to Nazareth. They thought that Jesus was with some of the others in the group, but when they looked for Him at the end of the first day, they couldn't find Him anywhere.

Frantic with worry, Mary and Joseph hurried back to Jerusalem. They searched high and low in the busy streets, but there was no sign of their son. Finally, on the third day, to their great relief, they found Him. He was in the Temple speaking about God to the learned religious teachers. The rabbis were listening to every word He said and were astonished at the wise things He was saying. And His parents were astonished at seeing Him there.

'My son, why have you treated us like this?' asked Mary. 'Your father and I have been searching for you in great anxiety.'

'Why were you searching?' Jesus asked in surprise. 'Did you not know I would be in my Father's house?'

His parents understood that 'my Father's house' referred to the Temple where God was worshipped, but they were puzzled by His question and the fact that He expected them to have known where He was. Again, Mary kept His words in her heart and remembered them.

Teaching and Troubles

As Jesus grew up, everyone was surprised at His great wisdom and compassion. He was always helping people who were troubled or ill, and He also began telling people about new teachings from God, which were sometimes different from the old ones they were used to. For example, they had previously been taught that it was all right to hit someone who hit them, but Jesus said: 'Now when people hit you, you should not hit them back, but turn the other cheek and forgive them.'

Some of the religious leaders were already jealous of Jesus because people were listening to Him rather than to them, and they began to speak angrily against Him. As their anger grew and their complaints became more and more serious, Mary's heart began to sink. She remembered the words of Simeon in the Temple when Jesus was one year old – how he had prophesied that people would not believe her son and how much He would suffer in the future.

Mary's cousin Elizabeth had a son who was a few months older than Jesus. He was known as John the Baptist and he was also being attacked by the priests because he was preaching about the coming of a new Holy One from God. John was telling everyone to repent and have their sins washed away in the River Jordan so they would recognize the Holy One when He appeared. The Holy One, of course, was Jesus.

There was another King Herod on the throne by this time. He was called Herod Antipas and he was just as cruel as his father, Herod the Great. When he heard about the preaching of John the Baptist, he became frightened. By killing all the baby boys who were in the area around Bethlehem, his father had hoped that the Holy One the wise men had spoken about had also been killed, but it seemed that the plan had failed. In a fury, Herod Antipas ordered his soldiers to cut off John the Baptist's head because of the things he was saying. So they did.

After this happened to Elizabeth's son, Mary feared even more for the safety of Jesus; but He continued to teach, and even told His followers that He was the Holy One whom John had been preaching about.

The priests muttered angrily among themselves and decided that Jesus should also be killed.

Mary at the Cross

Jesus was on His way once again to the yearly Passover festival in Jerusalem. This would be the last one He would attend. His mother, Mary, and His disciples were with Him. As He rode into the town on a donkey, people waved palm leaves and shouted, 'Blessings on Him who comes in the name of the Lord!'

But not everyone was so welcoming. The kindly Zacharias, who had been the high priest when Jesus was a child, had long since died, and the new high priest wanted Jesus killed. He persuaded the Roman governor to have Him crucified.

Jesus was taken outside the town and beaten and hung on a cross to die. His mother wept as she watched. All the words that Simeon had said in the Temple over 30 years before had come true. As well as speaking about the future sufferings of Jesus, she remembered how he had said to her, 'And you too shall be pierced to the heart.'

Jesus looked down with compassion at His mother, who stood weeping at the foot of the cross. One of His disciples was standing by her side. Jesus lovingly told her, 'Mother, there is your son,' meaning the disciple. Then He said to the disciple, 'There is your mother,' meaning Mary.

And the disciple understood that Jesus wanted him to be as a son to Mary and to look after her. Mary's husband, Joseph, was already dead, and Jesus knew that when He died she would have no one to take care of her.

The name of this beloved disciple was John. He and his brother had become believers when they were fishermen and had heard Jesus preaching near the Sea of Galilee.

After the death of Jesus, the disciples and a few other followers gathered to pray in the upstairs room of a house in Jerusalem, and Mary was with them.

When Mary became pregnant with Jesus, people condemned her because she was not yet married. They did not believe her story about Jesus having been conceived through the Holy Spirit. It was a huge test and there was no way she could prove her innocence. She is now known as the Virgin Mary and worshipped and loved by millions of people around the world, and many pray to her to help them with their troubles.

Fátimih's Story
(c. 604 – 633 AD)
'lady of light'

The Blessed One

'Is it a girl or a boy?' the maids asked when they heard the sound of the newborn baby crying.

They hoped it was a boy. Nearly everyone at that time hoped for boys. It was a shocking thing to happen, but some of the wild tribes in the desert even used to kill their baby girls as soon as they were born because they thought boys were better. The maids knew that wouldn't happen in this household though, because the baby's father was the Prophet Muhammad and He said that girls were as important as boys in the sight of God. But they couldn't help secretly hoping it was a boy because three daughters had already been born into the family and only one son.

When Muhammad heard the news that His fifth child had been born and that she was a girl, He was delighted. Although He loved all His children, there was a special spiritual bond between Him and this little one. He and His wife named the baby Fátimih, which means 'safe from fire', hoping she would be protected from tests. She is also known as the Blessed, the

Righteous, the Luminous, the Chaste and the Pure One.

Muhammad and His wife did have three little boys after Fátimih was born, but they all died when they were young. And, sadly, Fátimih's older brother also died. She was very fond of her three big sisters, but, as they came of age, they married and left home, and she missed them greatly. However, there was a boy called Zayd who lived with them as one of the family. He had been a slave but Muhammad made him free and then adopted him.

There was also a little boy called 'Alí whom Fátimih played with. He was a young cousin of her father and had come to live with the family when he was five years old and Fátimih was four. 'Alí was a kind and spiritual boy who was greatly blessed and trusted by Muhammad when he grew up.

Love for Her Father

It soon became clear that Fátimih was no ordinary child. Although she was usually timid and shy, there was something special about her and she was very close to her father. It is said that when He left the house, He always said goodbye to her last of all so she would be in His presence for as long as possible, and that when He returned, she would be the first to welcome Him home. When she was five years old and her mother explained to her that Muhammad was a Messenger of God, Fátimih loved Him even more. One of the things she liked to do was to go with her father when He went to a holy place called the Ka'bah to pray.

The Ka'bah was believed to have been a holy place since the time of Adam. Abraham and His son Ishmael had built

37

onto this shrine and people had been praying there ever since. Through her father, Fátimih was descended from Abraham and Ishmael so this made it especially important to her. Inside the building was a black stone, which people believed had come to earth from Paradise. At the end of each day, when the men finished their work, they looked forward to walking around this building saying their prayers before going home.

As well as accompanying her father when He went to pray at the Ka'bah, Fátimih also went with Him to secret meetings with His followers. She would hold His hand tight as they hurried through the narrow streets, hoping no one would see where they were going. There were many who opposed Muhammad and the teachings He had brought from God. It wasn't safe for His followers to meet openly with Him as they were likely to be attacked.

Although many people at the time believed in God, they also believed in idols. In fact, there were a whole lot of idols and the people worshipped three goddesses in particular. People were very attached to these goddesses and didn't want to listen to anything new. Also, the tribe Muhammad belonged to, which was called the Quraysh, had split into different clans and all of them strongly opposed Him. One of these clans was the keeper of some highly revered idols which were kept inside the Ka'bah itself. This clan especially did not want anything to change.

Among the things Muhammad told His followers at these meetings was that they should worship only the one God, who was almighty and all-knowing; that every believer was equal before God; and that they should be kind to strangers. He also said that they should believe in all the Prophets and Great Ones of the past, including Abraham, Moses and Jesus.

Attacks

One day, when Fátimih was about nine years old, she was with her father in a place of prayer outside the town. Muhammad was praying with His head bowed to the ground when a gang of men from one of the clans of His own tribe surrounded Him and threw the smelly insides of a slaughtered animal over Him. Muhammad continued His prayer as Fátimih removed the bits and pieces from His clothes. When she finished, she turned to face the gang of ignorant clansmen and fiercely scolded them for being so rude and disrespectful. They hadn't expected this from the normally shy little girl! They didn't say a word and Muhammad was able to finish His prayer in peace.

On another day, she was with her father at the Ka'bah when a group of men from the same clan as before tried to strangle Muhammad by wrapping His clothes around His neck. Fátimih shouted for help and a man called Abu Bakr came running over and managed to stop them. But then they turned on Abu Bakr and beat him up instead.

When Fátimih was 12 years old, the persecution became so fierce that the Holy Family was forced to leave Mecca and live outside the town in a small ravine that was closed in by hills on three sides and could only be reached by a narrow path. The food soon ran out and the crying of hungry children could be heard several miles away in Mecca.

For three years Muhammad and His family and the believers suffered from hunger and thirst and also from the scorching sun in summer and the bitter cold in winter. The Quraysh made it almost impossible for anyone to take food or clothing to them. But some of the people who secretly believed in Muhammad found a way: they loaded food and other necessary items onto the backs of horses and camels, pointed the animals in the direction of the camp and sent them off one at a time along the path, hoping they wouldn't stop until they got there.

No sooner had this time of suffering ended than another sad thing happened. Fátimih's mother died. Fátimih wept bitterly and became so weak it was thought she might die too. Muhammad was also heartbroken at the death of His beloved wife, and Fátimih knew she must now give even greater support to her father.

Soon after the death of her mother, some men threw earth over her father's head, and Fátimih couldn't help crying when she saw Him coming into the house covered in mud. But Muhammad smiled and said: 'Do not cry, my daughter, for God shall protect your father.'

The love of Muhammad for Fátimih became greater day by day. When He saw her coming towards Him, He would stand up, kiss her on the forehead and seat her next to Himself. He said: 'Whoever pleased Fátimih has indeed pleased God, and whoever has caused her to be angry has indeed angered God. Fátimih is a part of me. Whatever pleases her pleases me, and whatever angers her angers me.'

Forced to Leave

Eventually things became so difficult for the family that they left the Mecca area and went to live in the small town of Medina, 280 miles away. Gradually, hundreds of Muhammad's followers from Mecca came to live there too.

However, that wasn't the end of the troubles. Fátimih's three sisters were married and still living in Mecca. Their husbands belonged to clans which were still opposed to Muhammad, and the men were under a great deal of pressure from their families and clan leaders to divorce their wives. The husband of Zaynab, who was Fátimih's oldest sister, loved his wife and didn't want to divorce her, but she was a Muslim and he and his clan weren't, and he was worried someone would kill her if she stayed in Mecca. He reluctantly agreed she should go to Medina to live with her own family where she would be safe. Later, he also became a Muslim and they were happily reunited once more.

The husband of Fátimih's second oldest sister, Ruqiyyah, gave in to the pressure from his clan and divorced his wife. Fátimih was pleased to be with her sister again, although she was sorry it had happened in such an unhappy way.

But when the clan leaders tried to bribe the husband of Fátimih's third sister, Umm Kulthum, and persuade him to divorce his wife, he refused.

'I love my wife deeply and I have a great and high esteem for her father, even though I have not entered the religion of Islam,' he said.

Marriage and Children

When Fátimih was about 20 years old, her cousin 'Alí, whom she had played with as a child, asked to see Muhammad. He wished to ask for permission to marry Fátimih, but at first he was so over-awed to be asking such an important thing that he couldn't speak! Fátimih was known as the Pure and Luminous One and 'Alí knew that other men had asked to marry her but she had refused. As 'Alí stood tongue-tied in front of Him, Muhammad guessed what he wished to ask and gladly gave His consent. In fact, He was delighted, for He loved 'Alí and knew that Fátimih did too.

Muhammad prayed: 'O Lord, bless them both, bless their house and bless their children.'

Fátimih was very happy, even though the work of the house was hard. 'Ali worked as a water-carrier – filling bucket after bucket with water from a well and delivering it to different houses – while Fátimih ground corn to make bread until her hands were sore and her body ached. But she knew that there were many even poorer than they were, and just as her father had done, she shared whatever she had with her neighbours.

One day, Fátimih's sister, Ruqiyyah, fell ill with a fever and died. Muhammad was away at the time, but as soon as He returned He visited her grave and Fátimih went with Him. As they sat on the edge of the grave, Fátimih couldn't stop crying and her father comforted her and dried her tears with the hem of His cloak.

This sad time was followed by a happy event. Fátimih and 'Alí's first child was born. It was a boy and he was named Hasan. The following year, another healthy son was born and he was called Husayn. Muhammad loved to play with His baby grandsons, and sometimes, it is said, they even climbed onto His back while He was saying His prayers but He never minded!

In the years that followed, Fátimih had four more children, although two of them died when they were very young. The two who lived were little girls, whom she named after two of her sisters.

More Attacks

Life was fairly peaceful for a while, but some of the Quraysh in Mecca were gathering their forces to attack Muhammad and His followers in Medina. One spring, the enemy set off with a large army of three thousand men and camels. On the way, a Bedouin tribe joined them. Eventually they came to a plain at the foot of a mountain called Mount Uhud, just three miles from Medina, and here they set up camp and prepared to attack the believers in the town.

Some of the other tribes in the area came to Muhammad's aid, but the fighting was very fierce and 74 of the believers were killed. Muhammad was injured and fell from His horse and news reached His family that He had been killed.

As soon as she heard this dreadful news, Fátimih ran in tears to the battlefield to find out if the report was accurate. With enormous relief, she saw Muhammad walking down the mountain to meet her. But her joy turned to distress when she saw He was bleeding heavily. She didn't have the kind of medicine we use today, so she burned a piece of straw matting and put the ashes on His wounds to heal them.

After several more battles, Muhammad was able to make a peace treaty with some of the Quraysh, and several young men in the tribe became Muslims.

The Appointment

One day Muhammad told Fátimih that He had a secret He wished to tell her, something that nobody else knew. He said the time had come for Him to leave this world. Later, when He became ill, He asked to see her. When Fátimih came to His bedside, He kissed her and whispered something in her ear, and she wept. Then He whispered again in her ear, and she smiled.

Her stepmother was watching and was curious to know what Muhammad had said. 'You cry and you laugh at the same time, Fátimih?' she queried. 'What did the Messenger of God say to you?'

Fátimih replied, 'He first told me that He would soon be meeting His Lord, and so I cried. Then He said to me, "Don't cry, for you will be the first of My family to join Me," so I laughed.'

Not long afterwards, Muhammad passed away, just as He had said. Fátimih was overcome with grief. Not only was Muhammad her dearly loved earthly father, but He was her spiritual father and had been her guide and comfort all of her life. Although Muhammad had told her not to cry, she couldn't help it. The Angel Gabriel came to her in a vision and whispered holy secrets in her ear to comfort her. Then, six months later, Fátimih also died. She was 29 years old.

It is said that Fátimih never laughed after the death of Muhammad until the day of her own death, but on that day she was very happy. She smiled at her husband, 'Alí, and said: 'I have an appointment today with the Messenger of God!'

Fátimih was devoted to her father and she understood from an early age that He was a Messenger of God. Even when she was a child, she bravely tried to protect Him from His enemies and was never afraid of telling them off! She was a great comfort to Him and brought Him great joy. She is loved by millions of Muslims, men and women alike, who praise her holy name and call her 'the Lady of Light'.

Táhirih's Story
(1817 – 1852)
'the Pure One'

When she was born, Táhirih was given the name of Fátimih Umm-Salamih. Many little Muslim girls were given the name of Fátimih in honour of Muhammad's holy daughter. Táhirih's family also called her Zarrín-Táj, 'Crown of Gold'. Later, when she was grown up, the enlightened religious teacher Siyyid Kázim called her Qurratu'l-'Ayn, which means 'Solace of the Eye'. Later still, Bahá'u'lláh and the Báb called her Táhirih, meaning 'the Pure One', and this is the name by which she is best known.

Behind the Curtain

It was stuffy and hot hiding behind the heavy curtain but Táhirih didn't mind. She was happy because she could hear everything her father was saying to his class of religious students and it was all very interesting. But although her father was a learned Muslim priest who was highly respected in Persia, Táhirih did not always agree with what he said, and this made her think about things for herself.

None of the students knew she was there. She sat without moving, cross-legged on the floor, quietly listening to their questions and her father's answers. She was not allowed to join the class. Only boys were supposed to be interested in serious matters. Even though the Prophet Muhammad had said a thousand years before that girls and boys were equal in the sight of God, not everyone believed it yet. The young male students would have been shocked to have a girl in their class, even if she were to be veiled and no one could see her face. No one except other women and the close members of Táhirih's family had been allowed to see her face after she reached the age of nine. Even husbands didn't always see the faces of their future wives until after they were married.

One day Táhirih was sitting behind the curtain as usual, listening as her father gave a talk about religion to a room full of men, when she heard him say something that wasn't quite right. Without thinking, she spoke out, telling him about the mistake. There was a shocked silence. Nobody except her father had known she was there. But what she said was so interesting, the religious scholars wanted to hear her views. After that, she was allowed to join in their discussions, as long as she stayed behind the curtain. Her fame spread throughout her hometown of Qazvín in Persia and everyone was talking about this remarkable little girl who understood more than the religious leaders.

Her father sighed. He knew this gifted daughter of his was cleverer than any of his students, although sometimes he wished she didn't ask so many awkward questions! She was always trying to find the meaning of the holy writings and the prophecies. Secretly, he was very proud of her but he wished she had been a boy instead of a girl.

'A boy would have brought fame to my family and succeeded me!' he said to his wife.

He never guessed what great things Táhirih would do in the future.

Meanwhile, Táhirih spent her time learning everything she could and listening to the most recent news, especially about religion. She had a feeling something exciting was about to happen.

Forbidden Books

It was the custom of the time for girls to be married young, so when Táhirih was 13 years old her parents arranged for her to be married to a cousin and her peaceful way of life came to an end.

This cousin was not a nice man. He was very prejudiced and disagreed with Táhirih's ideas about religion. They had two boys and a girl, but as the children grew older Táhirih's husband refused to allow her to spend much time with them in case she told them about her ideas. In the end, he took them away from her altogether. From then on, Táhirih spent most of her time in the house of her parents.

One day she was visiting another cousin when she noticed some interesting books in his library. They were written by an enlightened religious teacher called Shaykh Ahmad and were about the coming of the Promised One. Táhirih asked if she could borrow them.

Her cousin hesitated.

'Your father will not be pleased to see you reading these books,' he warned. 'He might even have me killed for lending them to you!' But in the end he agreed to lend the books to her and Táhirih took them home.

Books were still rare in those days. In Persia, they were usually written out by hand, so there were very few copies made. In the privacy of her room, Táhirih carefully turned the pages and felt her heart quicken in excitement. The books were all about the coming of a great one from God whom Muhammad and Jesus and Moses and all the other Messengers of God had promised would come with new teachings for the world. And, she read, the time of His coming was now!

It was impossible for Táhirih to remain silent about this exciting news. She told everyone, and her family and husband became very angry with her. She tried to discuss it with her father but he didn't understand. Shaykh Ahmad had passed away by then, so she wrote letters to his successor, Siyyid Kázim, asking many questions. He gave wonderful answers and she longed to meet him.

Eventually she persuaded her father to allow her to make a pilgrimage with her sister and others to Karbilá. This was where several Muslim shrines were and it also happened to be where Siyyid Kázim lived. Her father agreed because he hoped she would change her mind about these new ideas if she went to the holy shrines to pray.

As soon as possible Táhirih set off to cross the desert to Karbilá, in the neighbouring country of Iraq.

Finding the Promised One

Táhirih was bitterly disappointed when she arrived in Karbilá to find that Siyyid Kázim had died just ten days before. When she asked if he had left any instructions for his disciples and learned that he had said they should fast and pray to be guided to find the Promised One, she took herself off to a quiet place where she could pray and fast in private.

One night, just before dawn, she fell asleep and had a wonderful dream. She saw a radiant youth standing in the sky and surrounded by light. He was wearing a black cloak, and she knew He was descended from the Prophet Muhammad because He wore a green turban on His head. His hands were raised up towards the sky and He was reciting verses from God. In her dream, Táhirih memorized one of the verses. When she woke up she quickly wrote it down in her notebook.

Shortly after this, she heard that her sister's husband, who was also interested in these new teachings, was about to set off from his home in Qazvín to search for the Promised One.

Immediately, Táhirih sent a sealed letter to him and asked him to give it to the Promised One when he found Him. Her brother-in-law, Mírzá Muhammad 'Alí, promised he would.

She told him, 'Say to Him from me:

> The light of Thy face
> flashed forth,
> and the rays of thy face
> rose high.
> Then speak the word,
> 'Am I not your Lord?'
> and 'Thou art, Thou art!'
> we will all reply!

When Mírzá Muhammad 'Alí later arrived in Shiraz, in the

south of Persia, he was guided through prayer to recognize that a young man called the Báb was the Promised One. The Báb was a descendant of the Prophet Muhammad through His daughter Fátimih. As well as being a Messenger of God, He said He was the herald of one even greater than Himself who would appear within the next few years.

Mírzá Muhammad 'Alí gave the Báb the letter and message from Táhirih. The Báb lovingly welcomed Mírzá Muhammad 'Alí as the sixteenth person to believe in Him and said that Táhirih was the seventeenth. Not only was Táhirih one of the first 18 believers (who were called the 18 Letters of the Living by the Báb) but she was the only woman among them.

Later, when Táhirih was given some of the writings of the Báb to read, her heart quickened in wonder when she found the exact words He had said to her in her dream! At that moment she knew, without any doubt, that His message was true. She fell to her knees and bowed her head to the ground and thanked God for so great a bounty.

Táhirih was radiant with joy and began telling everyone in Karbilá that the Promised One had come. When she was teaching the men she still had to sit behind a curtain, but nothing stopped her and many men and women became believers.

Such excitement was caused that the religious leaders became jealous, saying she was taking people away from the true faith of God. Some people even threw stones at her. They were especially annoyed when she was seen wearing colourful clothes one day during the Muslim holy month of mourning, when everyone else wore black. But Táhirih was not being disrespectful – she was celebrating the anniversary of the birth of the Báb which fell on the same date.

Eventually, she received permission from the authorities to leave Karbilá and go to Baghdad, where she was ordered to stay until a decision was made about what to do with her!

Adventures on a Journey

About this time news came that the Báb had called all His followers to a conference in a small village called Badasht. Although the Báb was imprisoned in a castle in the far north of Persia at the time and it was impossible for Him to attend, He urged the believers to gather for this conference where something very important was going to happen.

Táhirih wondered how she would be able to go, especially as she was still in Baghdad and the governor had ordered guards to surround the house where she was staying to prevent her from leaving. Every time she looked out a window, there were the soldiers with their guns watching her every movement.

Then, to her relief, word came from the governor that the Sultan of Turkey had given permission for her to be set free, but only if she promised to leave the country. She immediately set off to cross the border back into Persia.

More than 30 of Táhirih's friends went with her, and as they travelled through the towns and villages, others joined their caravan. Wherever she stayed, streams of people came to hear her talk about the new Faith and each time the religious leaders became angry and ordered her to leave again. But in one area a chief was so impressed by her knowledge that he gave his permission when twelve thousand of his men volunteered to follow her to protect her! Táhirih thanked him but said the men should return home to their families. Her fame spread far and wide, not just as a beautiful and educated woman, but as a great speaker, poetess and defender of the rights of women.

But, again, it was the religious leaders who arose against her. They told lies to the mayor in one of the towns and he allowed a mob to rob Táhirih and her companions of all their belongings. They were taken out of the town and left in a field without transport, food or shelter. It was only when the governor of the region heard what had happened that they were rescued. He was furious with the mayor and the priests and tried to make it up to Táhirih by returning her possessions, animals and drivers. He wanted her to stay longer but she was in a hurry to get to the conference, so she travelled on.

In one town she was visited by ladies of high society and she was able to tell them too about the Faith. She also spoke with the religious leaders and their followers, and both Muslims and Jews became Bábís because of her teaching.

When she arrived in one of the villages, two of her brothers came to meet her. They said that her father wished to see her. Táhirih reluctantly agreed to return home for a few days. She loved her father and knew that he loved her too, but when she tried to explain to him about the divine station of the Báb, he still did not understand.

Rescued

Soon after her return, trouble broke out in Qazvín and one of Táhirih's uncles was killed. This uncle had been fiercely opposed to the teachings of Shaykh Ahmad and Siyyid Kázim. He had even hit Táhirih when she had tried to explain their teachings to him. When he was killed, she was blamed for his death. Many innocent believers were killed and the priests threatened to kill Táhirih too. Neither Táhirih nor any of the other believers had anything to do with the death of her uncle but the priests did not want to believe her. Her father locked her in her room and told some women to watch her closely to prevent her escaping.

It seemed, after all, that Táhirih would not be able to go to the conference called by the Báb. She was in despair and prayed to God for help. When she heard that the chief priest planned to kill her, she sent a message to him saying that before nine days had passed God would set her free. If this didn't happen, she added, the priest could carry out his threat and kill her.

It was Bahá'u'lláh who came to her rescue. He was at His house in Tehran at the time, and when He heard Táhirih was confined to her father's house in Qazvín and that she had said she would be freed within nine days, He made arrangements for her to be rescued.

There was a close friend of Táhirih, called Khátún-Ján, who lived in Qazvín. She and her family were also Bábís and she found ways to get into the house where Táhirih was imprisoned.

Sometimes Khátún-Ján disguised herself as a beggar. At other times she pretended to be a washer-woman who had come to help with the laundry. Nobody took any notice of her, and in this way she was able to get news to Táhirih and even to smuggle in food, for Táhirih suspected her husband was trying to poison her.

One day, in her disguise as a beggar, Khátún-Ján managed to get a letter to Táhirih. It was from Bahá'u'lláh and explained a plan for her to escape. An hour later, following the instructions in the letter, Táhirih managed to slip out of the house without being seen and meet her friend and her friend's husband outside.

They led Táhirih to a carpenter's house where nobody would think of looking for her. When night fell, Khátún-Ján's husband and a trusted friend took Táhirih to the high wall that surrounded the town and the three of them managed to slip through a gate without being seen. There, waiting for them on the other side, were three horses that Bahá'u'lláh had arranged for someone to bring from Tehran.

Under cover of darkness they rode to Tehran by a roundabout route so they wouldn't be noticed, and the following morning they safely arrived at the house of Bahá'u'lláh.

Back in Qazvín, people were searching all through the night for Táhirih but it seemed she had disappeared into thin air!

The Conference of Badasht

A few days later Bahá'u'lláh arranged for some friends to take Táhirih to the village of Badasht, where the conference was being held, and He followed shortly afterwards. Although the Báb was unable to be there because He was still in prison, Bahá'u'lláh arranged everything. He rented three gardens: one for Himself, another for Quddús (the eighteenth and last Letter of the Living), and the third for Táhirih and her attendant. There was also a large general area where tents were put up for the rest of the believers. Altogether, 81 believers gathered for the conference, which lasted for three weeks.

Bahá'u'lláh revealed a new Tablet every day and gave everyone a new name. This is when Táhirih was first given her name, which means 'the Pure One'. Everyone present worshipped her, she was so holy in their eyes. But something was about to happen that would be a big test and would shock them deeply.

Bahá'u'lláh was ill with a fever one day and could not come to the general meeting area, so Quddús told the believers to go to Bahá'u'lláh's garden instead. Everyone went except for Táhirih. She sent a message to Quddús saying that as Bahá'u'lláh was unwell, it would be better if Quddús and the others came to her garden.

Quddús disagreed. He sent a message back saying, 'This garden is preferable. Come, then, to this one.'

So Táhirih did – but not in the way that everyone expected. As she left her garden and walked towards them, they could hear her voice loudly proclaiming a verse from the Qur'án, the holy book of Muhammad:

The Trumpet is sounding! The great Trump is blown!
The universal Advent is now proclaimed!

Then, suddenly, there she was, standing at the entrance of Bahá'u'lláh's tent in front of everyone. And she was not wearing her veil! Everyone had heard that she was beautiful, but that day her face shone with a spiritual beauty and power that dazzled their eyes. But as well as being dazzled, they were horrified because it was considered such a dreadful sin for a man to see a woman's face, unless she was related to him. How was it possible that the pure Táhirih, whom everyone worshipped as a saint, was standing there without her veil?

Some of the men screamed and ran away to the hills. One even cut his throat and nearly died! Others were speechless with shock. But a few understood what was happening. An important point had been made: this was the time for new teachings from God and some of the old ways would eventually need to go, including women having to wear the veil.

Bahá'u'lláh sent some of the believers to find those who had run away. Most of them returned, although a few were still upset because of what Táhirih had done and they thought that Bahá'u'lláh should not have named her the Pure One. But when the Báb heard about their complaints He wrote a letter from His prison agreeing with the name Bahá'u'lláh had given her. In fact, the Báb had already called her Táhirih, the Pure (and Siddíqih, the Truthful), in a Tablet He had written about her several months before, when she was still in Iraq.

Every day an old law was changed and a new one took its place. By the end of the conference the friends understood for the first time that the Bábí Faith was a new revelation from God and not just part of the religion of Muhammad.

Martyrdom

After the conference everyone left to return to their homes. But the enemies of the Faith were waiting for them. Bahá'u'lláh was arrested and tortured before finally being released. Quddús was put under house arrest as soon as he reached his village. And Táhirih was arrested before she reached home. She was later taken by soldiers to Tehran and imprisoned for nearly four years in the house of the mayor. At first she was kept outside in the upper room of a barn. It could only be reached by a ladder, which was removed after food had been taken to her. This time, there was no way to escape.

But Táhirih did not mind. She was on fire with the love of the

Faith and very happy. The wife of the mayor became her dear friend and before long Táhirih was taken to stay in the house. Although she was usually kept locked in her bedroom, she was allowed visitors and many seekers came to ask her questions. Most of these visitors were friendly but there were some priests who came to argue with her and try to persuade her not to believe in the Báb. When they failed, they secretly plotted to kill her.

One day, when a wedding feast was being held in the house for the son of the mayor, Táhirih was invited to attend. The tables were laden with delicious food, and professional musicians were playing the sitar and singing. But the important lady guests were not interested in the food or the music. They just wanted to be with Táhirih. They crowded around her, listening with wonder as she told them about the Báb and explained the true meaning of the prophecies in the holy Qur'án.

Everyone loved to be with her. Even though she was a prisoner, several princesses came to the house to see her. It is said that the Shah of Persia himself wrote her a letter, saying he wished to marry her and make her the head of all his other wives, but only if she stopped believing in the Báb! Of course, she refused.

The Shah summoned her to his palace and asked her why she should believe in the Báb. In reply, Táhirih quoted a verse from the Qur'án, part of which said, 'To you be your Way, and to me mine.'

The Shah was silent when he heard these words. He knew what they meant. One thousand years before, Muhammad had said these very same words to people who refused to believe in the revelation He had brought from God. Now Táhirih was saying them to him because he refused to believe in the Báb. He bowed his head and left the room without saying another word.

The day following the visit to the palace, the mayor's wife went to Táhirih's room and was surprised to find her wearing a lovely dress of snow-white silk and the room fragrant with perfume.

'What is the reason for this dress and this perfume?' the mayor's wife asked.

Táhirih smiled as she answered, 'I am preparing to meet my beloved. I shall no longer be a prisoner in your home.'

By 'my beloved' Táhirih meant the Báb, who had been martyred two years before. It had not been possible for her to meet Him in this world but she knew that soon she would be meeting Him in the next.

The mayor's wife began to cry when she realized that Táhirih meant she was going to die.

'You must not cry,' Táhirih gently told her friend and mentioned a few things she wished to happen.

'My last wish,' she said, 'is that you do not allow anyone to come into my room until after I leave this house. No one must come to me while I am in my last prayers and devotions. This day I intend to fast – a fast which I shall not break until I am brought face to face with my beloved.'

The next night there was a knock on the door of the house. Outside was a group of soldiers. They had been sent by the priests who had secretly signed Táhirih's death warrant. The mayor and the police had been told but not the Shah, although he had recently given a general order to kill all Bábís. He only knew afterwards what had happened to Táhirih and was very upset when he heard. He had been deeply moved by her faith and greatly admired her knowledge.

The soldiers took Táhirih away under cover of darkness so no one would see what was happening. She was led to a garden on the outskirts of the town, where a drunken guard was ordered to kill her. Just before she died, it is said that she turned to the soldier in charge and said, 'You can kill me as soon as you like, but you cannot stop the emancipation of women!'

The mayor's son had followed Táhirih as she was being led away by the soldiers, and he saw and heard everything that happened. He ran back home with tears flowing down his face. When he told his mother how he had seen Táhirih being strangled with her own scarf and then buried in a disused well in the garden, she wept too.

But Táhirih's soul was radiantly happy, for at last she was with the Báb.

❧

Táhirih lived most of her life either under a veil or behind a curtain, and she was surrounded by prejudice against herself and all other women. Yet she still managed to tell thousands of people about the message of the Báb. She also recognized the future greatness of Bahá'u'lláh, although He did not declare His mission until after her death.

She became famous and loved in countries far beyond Persia for the great work she did in educating people about the equality of men and women. She gave inspiring talks and wonderful explanations about the holy writings. She was fearless and bold.

She wrote beautiful poems about the Báb and Bahá'u'lláh, and these are still recited and sung today. She had many tests, for even her children were taken away from her. But however difficult life became, her love for the Báb and her complete trust in God shone out like a beacon to give hope to men and women everywhere.

Bahíyyih Khánum's Story
(1846 – 1932)
'the Greatest Holy Leaf'

Through her father, Bahá'u'lláh, Bahíyyih Khánum was descended from Abraham and Sarah, as well as from Abraham's third wife, Katurah. She was also descended from the Prophet Zoroaster and the ancient Kings of Persia. Like Táhirih, when she was born she too had been named Fátimih after Muhammad's holy daughter, but later she was called Bahíyyih (Glorious) by Bahá'u'lláh.

In the Beginning

When Bahíyyih was a little girl she lived in a fine house in Persia, for her parents were rich. Princes and princesses used to come to their house as well as poor people who needed help. Followers of the Báb also came, including the great teacher Táhirih, who had converted hundreds of women in Persia to the new teachings of God proclaimed by the Báb. There were many other interesting people who visited their home but Bahíyyih was too young at the time to remember them all.

However, there was one thing she did remember all her life.

It was something that happened when she was six years old, her older brother, 'Abbás, was eight, and her little brother, Mihdí, was four.

It was the day their beloved father, Bahá'u'lláh, was put into prison because He believed in the Báb. The Báb had come with a new message from God and had announced that the Promised One of all religions would soon appear. His teachings had spread like wildfire through the country and there was great excitement everywhere, but the clergy were not happy because they didn't want to lose their power over the people. As soon as they could find an excuse, they were determined to kill every Bábí man, woman and child.

The excuse they were looking for came when a half-crazy young man shot at the Shah. The young man blamed the Shah for the martyrdom of the gentle Báb and also for allowing hundreds of the Báb's innocent followers to be killed and tortured. The Shah had been slightly hurt and the young man had been killed on the spot.

Bahá'u'lláh and the rest of the believers had nothing to do with this deed but one by one they were all arrested.

Within hours of Bahá'u'lláh's imprisonment, gangs gathered outside the family's house, shouting and throwing stones. With their mother, Navváb, the children fled for their lives, leaving everything behind. With the help of Bahíyyih's great-uncle Mírzá Yúsif (who was married to one of Bahá'u'lláh's aunts), they eventually found shelter in two small rooms in another part of the town where nobody knew them.

The house was close to the prison where Bahá'u'lláh was being kept. Every day they could hear the sound of the beating of drums getting louder and louder as a prisoner was taken out and killed. The children would cling to their mother in fear, never knowing whether the person being killed was their father or not. Rumours were flying around the city and it was impossible to know exactly what was happening.

Sometimes Bahíyyih had to be left alone in the house with her little brother while her mother and 'Abbás went to the great-uncle's house to get news. To make sure she wasn't seen, Navváb had to go when it was dark. Bahíyyih and Mihdí would sit, too frightened to move, until their mother returned. They did not dare light a lamp in case it was seen by someone passing outside.

'How well I remember cowering in the dark, with my little brother . . . in my arms,' Bahíyyih told a friend many years later.

Mihdí was too young to understand what was happening but Bahíyyih knew they were in great danger, although she didn't know exactly why. It seemed the whole town was hunting for them, and most of their friends and family had deserted them or were in hiding because they were frightened too.

With Her Father Again

One day Bahíyyih's great-uncle Yúsif discovered that there was a plot by the clergy to kill Bahá'u'lláh. Mírzá Yúsif was a Russian subject so he immediately went to the Russian Consulate in Tehran to ask for help in this matter. The head of the Consulate was an influential person and he promised to do what he could to protect Bahá'u'lláh. And he was as good as his word.

That night, great-uncle Yúsif came to the rooms where Navváb and her children were hiding and Bahíyyih listened in excitement to what he had to tell them. He said that the Russian Consul had stood up in the government court and said in a firm voice:

> Hearken to me! I have words of importance to say to you! Have you not taken enough cruel revenge? Have you not already murdered a large enough number of harmless people . . . ? How is it possible that you can even pretend to think that this august prisoner planned that silly attempt to shoot the Shah? . . . that stupid gun, used by that poor youth, could not have killed a bird. Moreover, the boy was obviously insane. You know very well that this charge is not only untrue, but . . . ridiculous.

And he warned them that if even one hair of the head of Bahá'u'lláh was harmed, there would be trouble!

Following this powerful speech, and four months after Bahá'u'lláh had first been imprisoned, the governor ordered His release. 'Abbás and Bahíyyih wept with joy when they heard this news from their great-uncle. And when they eventually saw their father, they immediately noticed there was something different about Him. He was still their beloved father but there seemed to be a glow about Him. They all saw it. It was as if something wonderful had happened since they had last seen Him.

It wasn't until some time later that they learned what it was. While Bahá'u'lláh had been chained in the darkness of the dungeon, an angel had appeared to Him in a vision. Pointing to His head, the angel had loudly proclaimed: 'By God! This is the Best-Beloved of the worlds . . . This is the Beauty of God amongst you . . .' And Bahá'u'lláh had felt the Holy Spirit of God flowing through Him, giving Him the knowledge of all things.

'I felt as if something flowed from the crown of My head over My breast, even as a mighty torrent . . . from the summit of a lofty mountain,' He later explained. 'Every limb of My body would, as a result, be set afire. At such moments My tongue recited what no man could bear to hear.'

Then, in a dream, God had told Bahá'u'lláh not to be afraid because of the cruel things that would happen to Him in the future, for He would raise up people to help Him – people who would be like the treasures of the earth.

Banishment

Bahá'u'lláh had been released from prison but the suffering of the Holy Family was not at an end. It was just beginning. Although He was ill because of the dreadful conditions in the prison, Bahá'u'lláh was ordered to leave Persia within the month and forbidden ever to return again.

On a cold January day in 1853, the family left Persia. Bahíyyih didn't mind where she lived, so long as she was with her adored father, and she must have breathed a sigh of relief when she knew she had been included with those who were going with Him. But when she looked around for her little brother, Mihdí, she was told he had to be left behind. He was not very strong and it was feared that he might die on the long, cold journey which lay ahead of them, so he had been left behind in the care of his great-grandmother.

This great-grandmother was the only person who came to see them off. Nobody else dared to come in case they were seen and arrested.

Bahíyyih found herself travelling through snow in the middle of winter on the way to Baghdad in the neighbouring land of Iraq. She was sitting with her mother in a small wooden carriage called a howdah, which was tied on the back of a mule. It was very uncomfortable. As the mule scrambled over the stony paths winding through the mountains, the howdah swayed from side to side like a ship, and Bahíyyih had to hold on tightly to stop herself being thrown about inside. It was bitterly cold and she shivered as icy winds blew through the cracks in the howdah and through her thin cotton clothes.

When each night fell, the Holy Family slept in inns in villages near the roadside. They would often be given a cold, bare room to sleep in, with no beds or means to light a fire to cook a meal. Navváb had already sold her jewellery and other belongings to pay for the expenses of the journey but the money from these soon ran out. Once, the only food she had to give to Bahíyyih and her brother was a little dry flour, which she put in the palms of their hands.

In Baghdad

After travelling for three months the family arrived at the Persian border, where Ottoman soldiers met them and escorted them to Baghdad.

At first they lived in another small house with just two rooms. One of the rooms was used by Bahá'u'lláh, while Bahíyyih and 'Abbás slept in the other with their mother, who was expecting another baby. Shortly after they arrived, the baby was born. It was a sweet little boy. Everyone was delighted and Bahíyyih helped her mother look after him.

Female guests were also entertained in this room, and many Arab women came, asking questions about the Báb. When Táhirih, the famous follower of the Báb, had been living in Baghdad several years before, she had told these women about the Báb and His teachings. They had become very interested and now wanted to know more. At the time, Bahá'u'lláh was just known as an important follower of the Báb and had not yet told people that He was the Manifestation of God whom the Báb said would appear after Him.

Once when an old lady visited the house, Bahíyyih wanted to help by making the tea. She was only about seven years old at the time and not very strong but she managed to carry a heavy samovar full of water up the steep stairs to her mother's room. When the water boiled, she served everyone with small glasses of hot, sweet tea. The old woman was very impressed and said, 'One proof that the Bábí teaching is wonderful is that a very little girl served the samovar!'

Bahá'u'lláh laughed and said to His small daughter, 'Here is the lady converted by seeing your service at the samovar!'

A few months later the family moved to a larger house and many people came to see Bahá'u'lláh, for His fame had spread far and wide. However, there were many who were jealous and opposed Him, particularly his half-brother who was called Mírzá Yahyá. To prevent any disunity, the following year Bahá'u'lláh left Baghdad to pray and meditate in the remote mountains of Kurdistan.

He was away for two years and during this time Mírzá Yahyá

lived with the family and wouldn't allow anyone to visit the house. The uncle was frightened the authorities would discover he was there, so he refused to allow any children to come to play with Bahíyyih. When he saw her peeping round the door at two little girls of her own age who lived in the next house, he immediately slammed the door shut and locked it. Saddest of all, he even refused to let a doctor come to the house when her sweet baby brother fell ill. When the baby died, nobody knew where he was taken to be buried.

Life was especially hard for Bahá'u'lláh's wife, Navváb, who was not used to doing heavy housework, and the uncle never offered to help. During this sad and lonely time, Bahíyyih helped her mother fetch bucket after bucket of water from a deep well in the house until her hands were sore from the rough, wet ropes and her arms were aching.

To everyone's relief, after some time the cowardly uncle went to live in a house of his own, although the Holy Family still cooked his food and sent it round to him, for Bahá'u'lláh had said to treat him with kindness.

While she waited for her father to return, Bahíyyih helped her mother make a fine red coat for Him out of small pieces of cloth that Navváb had brought with her from Persia.

Happiness

One day, when Bahíyyih was 11 and 'Abbás was 13, news came that Bahá'u'lláh was on His way home to Baghdad.

Bahíyyih was sitting with her mother and brother, waiting for her beloved father to arrive. They heard a footstep outside. The door opened. A dervish, burnt brown by the sun and dressed in a long brown robe, came into the room. Under the long beard and roughly-woven clothes the children recognized their father and ran into His arms and hugged Him.

'I could never forget this scene, so touching and so happy,' Bahíyyih told one of the friends many years later when she was remembering that happy time. 'Our joy cannot be described as we clung to him. I can see now my beloved mother, calm and gentle, and my brother holding his father's hand fast, as though never again could He let Him go out of His sight . . .'

There was just one thing missing to make Bahíyyih completely happy. It was five years since she had last seen her little brother, Mihdí. She missed him deeply and must often have wondered if she would ever see him again. Then, after another two years had passed, when Mihdí was 11 years old, he was brought by a relative from Tehran to Baghdad. He was as gentle and kind as his brother, 'Abbás, and everybody loved him.

Time to Leave

The Holy Family had been living in Baghdad for ten years when, without warning, the Ottoman authorities summoned Bahá'u'lláh to the capital city of Turkey to be questioned at the court of the Sultan.

The townsfolk were very upset at this news. They didn't want the Holy Family to leave. Although people did not fully understand the divine station of Bahá'u'lláh, they loved Him as their friend and helper and because of His great knowledge and wisdom. They also greatly respected His eldest son, 'Abbás, whom Bahá'u'lláh now called 'the Master'.

Hundreds of people living in Baghdad flocked to the house to say goodbye. There were so many it was difficult for the family to get on with the packing, so Bahá'u'lláh accepted the offer of a friendly official to stay for several days in a large and beautiful garden on the other side of the River Tigris. Large tents were put up for the believers and a stream of people came from the town to see Him for the last time.

While Bahá'u'lláh was staying in the garden He declared for the first time that He was the Manifestation of God whom Moses, Jesus, Muhammad, the Báb and other Messengers of God had promised would come to bring peace to the world. Because of this declaration, the garden became known as the Garden of Riḍván (Paradise).

Bahíyyih's brothers had been among those who went to the garden with Bahá'u'lláh, while she stayed behind to help her mother with the last of the packing. The plan was that they would shortly follow but a gale blew up and the river flooded and they had to wait until the ninth day before they were able to go.

On the twelfth day, three days after Bahíyyih and her mother arrived in the garden, the whole family, plus some of the friends, left Baghdad on the first part of their journey to Constantinople (now called Istanbul), the capital city of Turkey.

Bahíyyih Khánum was now a beautiful young woman of 16. She had golden-brown hair and large, grey-blue eyes. She had a gentle sense of humour and was very intelligent. In the years that followed, several young men asked for her hand in marriage. But whenever Bahá'u'lláh asked her if she wished to marry, she always said no. Her wish was to be free to help her parents and brothers during all the troubles she knew they would have to face in the future. Bahá'u'lláh accepted her wish and lovingly said, 'Upon her rest the glory of My name and the fragrance of My shining robe.' Bahíyyih means 'Glorious'.

The Holy Family had been in Constantinople for only four months when they were sent to Adrianople (modern day Edirne) in the north of Turkey. It was here that Bahíyyih's jealous uncle Mírzá Yahyá poisoned Bahá'u'lláh, who nearly died. Even after this, Bahá'u'lláh was kind to him but Mírzá Yahyá continued to cause trouble. He said everyone should listen to him and not to Bahá'u'lláh, and he called a meeting in a mosque so people could hear both of them speak and decide whom they should follow.

On the day of the meeting Bahá'u'lláh went to the mosque but Mírzá Yahyá didn't turn up. Instead, he hid in his room. He knew that if he went everyone would find out how ignorant he was. When he had made the suggestion about holding the meeting he had never expected that Bahá'u'lláh would accept! Mírzá Yahyá knew his knowledge was as nothing compared to the divine knowledge of Bahá'u'lláh.

Bahíyyih Khánum became so unhappy at the actions of her cowardly uncle and the sadness he was causing her father that she couldn't eat or sleep and became as thin as a shadow.

After spending nearly five sorrow-filled years in Adrianople, Bahá'u'lláh and the believers were banished by the Ottoman government to the grim prison-city of 'Akká. Fortunately, Mírzá Yahyá didn't go with them – he was sent to Cyprus instead.

The Prison-City

The boat stopped in the rubbish-filled sea that was swirling around the walls of the prison-city of 'Akká. Sailors ordered the Holy Family and the believers to leave the boat and wade through the shallow water to the shore. Some of the sailors began to carry the women ashore on their backs but the Master told them to wait until he could find a chair so they could be carried with dignity over the water. They were then all led through the narrow streets to the prison, where the heavy doors slammed shut behind them.

It was stifling hot and the smell was so bad Bahíyyih Khánum fainted. The friends looked around for some clean water to give her to drink but all they could find was a muddy puddle of water being used by one of the prisoners to soften the straw he was making into mats. They strained some of this water and put it to Bahíyyih Khánum's lips in the hope of reviving her but the bad smell made her faint again.

Everyone became ill during the first few months they were crowded together in the prison cells. Two years passed and it seemed that the world had forgotten they were there. Then, to add to their sorrows, as Bahíyyih's brother Mihdí was praying on the flat roof of the prison, he fell through a skylight and was badly injured. The next day he died.

Bahá'u'lláh comforted everyone and revealed beautiful prayers about Mihdí, saying how blessed and pure he was and that through the sacrifice of his life God would bring unity to the world. Bahá'u'lláh called him the Purest Branch in the Cause of God.

Bahíyyih Khánum tearfully gathered the blood-stained clothes of her brother. Over the years she also collected strands of Bahá'u'lláh's hair from His comb and made them into lovely patterns which were later framed. The clothes of Mírzá Mihdí and a few locks of Bahá'u'lláh's hair are among other interesting and precious things related to the history of the Bahá'í Faith that can be seen in a museum on Mount Carmel in the Holy Land.

Four months after the death of Mihdí, parts of the prison were needed to house soldiers because a war had broken out. The Holy Family and the Bahá'ís with them were taken to live in different houses in the town. But they still were not free, for the whole town was a prison.

The Town Jail

One of the houses belonged to a Christian merchant called 'Údí Khammár and this is where Bahá'u'lláh's family and others eventually lived.

The house was on the upper floor and very small. As many as 13 people had to sleep in one of the rooms. It was also very noisy. The ground floor, under the rooms where they were living, was a public area where merchants conducted their business and people came and went all day long. Outside in the busy square, the shouts of boys and men selling bread or cheese or fruit or olives filled the air as soon as it was light. And the constant sound of women calling and children crying came through the open windows of the houses nearby.

For many years the only view Bahíyyih Khánum had was of the grey buildings in the square outside. And even these could only be seen through rows of tiny holes in the heavy wooden shutters on the windows, which allowed some light in but prevented people outside from seeing anyone inside the house. It was considered immoral for a man in the street to be able to see a woman looking out of her window.

But despite the overcrowding and the noise and the difficult conditions, there was a deep feeling of peace in the house, especially in the room of Bahá'u'lláh.

Then, suddenly, for three horrifying days, this peace was rudely interrupted.

Bahá'u'lláh was in the middle of dictating a Tablet when angry cries were heard outside. Dozens of soldiers with drawn swords had surrounded the house. Bahá'u'lláh and the Master were arrested and thrown into the town jail because a few believers had broken the law of God and the law of the land. Because of the wrong deeds of these few, many of the other believers, who were completely innocent, were being rounded up and locked in the jailhouse.

Bahá'u'lláh later wrote: 'My captivity can bring on Me no shame. Nay, by My life, it conferreth on Me glory. That which can make Me ashamed is the conduct of such of My followers as profess to love Me, yet in fact follow the Evil One.'

Bahíyyih Khánum was heart-broken at the sadness being caused to her beloved father and brother. Sometime after this event she visited the town jail to see for herself what it was like and she was shocked when the guards told her of the terrible conditions that had existed at the time of the arrests – how prisoners had been chained together as they lay on the dirty floor and a jailer had used whips knotted with lead to hit anyone who dared cry out or move. It was too unbearable to think about.

A few hours after Bahá'u'lláh and the Master had been arrested, an order was given for the house to be searched for weapons. As the ladies were completely on their own with no man to protect them, the Master did not want them to be alone when the soldiers came and He insisted that He be there as well. After some persuasion, the soldiers reluctantly agreed but they demanded that He come in chains.

When they arrived at the house, 'Abdu'l-Bahá tried to cover the chains with His cloak so that His mother would not see them and become upset. But she did see them and she wept bitterly. The soldiers didn't find any weapons, of course, and after a few days Bahá'u'lláh and the Master were found to be innocent and released from jail.

But the man who lived next door strengthened the wall between his house and the house of the Holy Family because he was frightened he would be attacked!

A Wedding

Life gradually returned to normal. Even the neighbour who had reinforced his wall came to realize he had been wrong to worry, and he and his wife became friendly with the Holy Family.

Now things had settled down, Bahíyyih Khánum and her mother decided it would be a good idea if the Master were to marry. At first He refused to even think of doing so because of the difficult conditions they were living in, but in the end He agreed. A lovely and sweet-natured girl arrived from Persia. Bahá'u'lláh named her Munírih (the Illumined One). However, there was just one problem preventing the couple from getting married: there was no spare room in the house for the Master and His future wife. The months went by and still the wedding date could not be set.

The neighbour, whose name was Ilyás 'Abbúd, kept asking his wife why the marriage of the Master and Munírih had not yet taken place. His wife asked Bahíyyih Khánum, who explained the situation. When 'Abbúd was told, he immediately offered to open a door in the wall between the two houses and give one of his rooms to the Master and His bride.

Bahíyyih Khánum and her mother made a simple white dress and head covering for Munírih to wear. Then, at nine one evening, Bahíyyih Khánum took her into the presence of Bahá'u'lláh. He warmly welcomed Munírih into the family and told her that the treasures of earth and heaven could not compare with the bounty of being the wife of the Master. An hour later, the wedding ceremony took place.

'Abbúd and his family eventually moved to a mansion outside the town. Now, as well as renting the first house, which had always been too small for them all, the Holy Family were able to rent 'Abbúd's house, which was much bigger. The two houses became one, joined by a small courtyard, and became known as the house of 'Abbúd.

It was in this house that Bahíyyih Khánum's nine nephews and nieces were born. She was able to help her sister-in-law look after these little ones, which must have made her very happy as she had never married to have children of her own. She was also there to comfort Munírih when five of the children died.

One of Bahíyyih's nephews was an especially sweet little boy. His name was Husayn and when he was four years old, he loved to go for walks through the fields, holding the hand of his grandfather, Bahá'u'lláh. When he returned home from these walks and was asked where he had been, he always said that he had been 'seeing things'. Sadly, little Husayn was one of the children who died and Bahá'u'lláh wrote on his tombstone that he was now 'seeing things' in all the worlds of God.

This house is also where Bahíyyih Khánum's mother passed away. Bahá'u'lláh was with His wife when she died and He said they would be together in all the realms of God forever.

Bahá'u'lláh had called His beloved wife 'the Most Exalted Leaf' and now He gave this title to His daughter, Bahíyyih Khánum. She is called 'the Greatest Holy Leaf', which has the same meaning.

Bahá'u'lláh lovingly told His daughter: 'We have . . . granted thee, in My court, a station such as none other woman hath surpassed.'

The Ascension of Bahá'u'lláh

Eight years after the death of His wife Bahá'u'lláh became ill with a fever. For some time He had been living in a house in the country, in an area known as Bahjí, outside 'Akká, while Bahíyyih Khánum and the Master stayed in the town looking after the affairs of the Faith and the pilgrims.

Bahá'u'lláh sent a messenger on horseback with a letter addressed to the Master, saying, 'I am not well, come to Me and bring Khánum.'

The Master and Bahíyyih Khánum went at once. Five days later the rest of the family living in 'Akká joined them. Bahá'u'lláh called the believers to His bedside and told them, 'I am very pleased with you all.' And He said that the Master would take care of the family, the friends and the Cause after His death.

Several days later, His soul ascended to the heavenly realms of God.

Although Bahá'u'lláh was still with her in a spiritual way

and her heart was full of the fragrance of His love, Bahíyyih Khánum couldn't help feeling deep despair knowing that she wouldn't see Him again in this world. She loved her father with all her heart and knew how much He loved her too.

He had revealed a Tablet for her, saying:

> How sweet thy presence before Me;
> how sweet to gaze upon thy face,
> to bestow upon thee My loving-kindness,
> to favour thee with My tender care,
> to make mention of thee in this, My Tablet . . .

The Holy Secret

Bahíyyih Khánum was sitting quietly in her room in 'Akká. For some years now, the family had been living in a larger house, just down the road from the house of 'Abbúd.

The house was usually buzzing with activity and laughter and people, for not only the Holy Family and their children lived there but also several widows and orphans. However, on this particular day it was very peaceful. The only sound was the rhythmic lap of the sea against the walls of the prison-city and the room was hazy with sunlight.

The door was half open and the children whispered as they passed Bahíyyih Khánum's room. Some paused to peep inside. Others gently knocked and Bahíyyih Khánum smiled and welcomed them in. They wondered why she spent so much time in her room praying but they didn't think it would be polite to ask. They were expected to take off their shoes before they entered the room out of respect for Khánum because she

79

was the daughter of Bahá'u'lláh. But there was another reason which they didn't know about at the time.

The secret was a casket containing the holy body of the Báb, which was hidden in her room. The Master knew this was the only safe place to hide it. For nearly 50 years the blessed body of the Báb had been moved from place to place after He had been martyred because the enemies of the Faith would not allow it to be buried. Eventually, it had secretly been brought by boat to 'Akká, and, when it was dark, smuggled through the narrow streets to the house, where it was kept for several years. But there were spies here too, so it was important to find somewhere safe to keep the sacred remains until they could be properly buried on Mount Carmel. And where safer than in the room of Bahíyyih Khánum?

Safe in Her Hands (1)

Bahíyyih Khánum's story does not end in 'Akká. The family later moved across the bay to Haifa, where she was able to serve the Faith in two more very important ways.

One had to do with the Master (who now asked to be called 'Abdu'l-Bahá, 'the Servant of Bahá'u'lláh').

In 1908 the prisoners were freed and a few years later 'Abdu'l-Bahá began His travels to America and Europe to spread the teachings of Bahá'u'lláh.

While He was away, 'Abdu'l-Bahá knew the Cause of God would be safe in the hands of Bahíyyih Khánum. He knew she would look after everyone, including His young grandson Shoghi Effendi, whose life was in danger from the enemies of the Faith. In fact, if Bahíyyih Khánum hadn't been there to take care of things, it would have been impossible for 'Abdu'l-Bahá to have left the Holy Land and travel to the West.

In a letter, 'Abdu'l-Bahá called Bahíyyih Khánum, 'My sister and beloved of my soul!'

Safe in Her Hands (2)

The second very important service Bahíyyih Khánum was able to offer during the last years of her life came after the passing of her brother, 'Abdu'l-Bahá, in 1921.

In His will 'Abdu'l-Bahá had appointed His grandson Shoghi Effendi to be the Guardian of the Cause of God. 'Abdu'l-Bahá told the friends to obey Shoghi Effendi and to take the greatest care of him. And this is exactly what Bahíyyih Khánum did.

But there was no time to recover from the great sadness caused by the death of 'Abdu'l-Bahá before something happened that shocked everyone – the disloyal great-uncles of Shoghi Effendi stole the keys to the Shrine of Bahá'u'lláh.

It was eight months before a government court ordered the keys to be returned to Shoghi Effendi. He was so grief-stricken at the wicked things these uncles were doing that he became ill. Leaving everything under the care of Bahíyyih Khánum, he travelled to Germany to see a doctor and then went on to Switzerland to spend time in the peace and solitude of the mountains.

'. . . his sensitive heart could bear it no more,' wrote Bahíyyih Khánum in a letter to the Bahá'ís.

Over the next few years Shoghi Effendi returned several times to these mountains where he could be alone and pray to God.

While Shoghi Effendi was away, Bahíyyih Khánum again

looked after the believers and protected the Faith from the actions of the enemies. And although she was now old and frail, she continued to write inspiring letters to the Bahá'ís throughout the world, encouraging them to be united and loving and to obey the teachings of Bahá'u'lláh.

'Dear friends!' she wrote in one of these letters, 'this is the day of faithfulness; this is the day of unity; this is the day of service. Let us not wait . . . let us arise in utmost love and harmony . . .'

A Heavenly Welcome

There was always a feeling of love around Bahíyyih Khánum. Many pilgrims spoke of it when they had been in her presence. It was as though her thoughts were in heaven even though she was still on earth.

She was constantly giving a gift to someone or other – usually something small, like an embroidered handkerchief or a handful of sweets, but given with such love that the person receiving it would be filled with a warm glow of happiness. The year before she passed away, a pilgrim from the West was very touched when she too was given a gift from the hand of Bahá'u'lláh's daughter. It was a ring with the symbol of the Greatest Name of God engraved upon a small red stone that glowed in the sun.

It was a night in the summer of 1932 when Bahíyyih Khánum died. She was buried in a beautiful garden on the side of Mount Carmel and her grave was covered in flowers. Hundreds of people came to her funeral. The sweet sound of chanting rose into the air and their hearts filled with love as they thought of Bahá'u'lláh's holy daughter.

Meanwhile, in the next world, there was great rejoicing.

Shoghi Effendi said that the maids of heaven circled around her soul, welcoming her with shouts of joy and calling aloud, 'Well done! Well done! Upon thee be God's blessings, O Most Exalted Leaf!' And he said that all of God's Prophets were there to greet her.

❧

No wonder Bahá'u'lláh said to His beloved daughter, 'How sweet to gaze upon thy face!' And 'Abdu'l-Bahá exclaimed, 'My sister and beloved of My soul!' And Shoghi Effendi called her 'the Most Exalted, the pure, the holy, the immaculate, the brightly shining Leaf'.

Bahíyyih Khánum had been blessed with being in the presence of Bahá'u'lláh and bathed in His love from the moment she had been born. And while most of the time she had been a prisoner, one way or another, her life was never dull. While other young girls were preparing to get married and live quiet, normal lives, she was with her family being exiled from place to place, never knowing from one day to the next whether they would all be martyred or not.

And although she became sad when she remembered some of the things that had happened in her life, she never complained about losing her home and her toys when she was six; or being hungry and cold on the long ride through the snowy mountains to Baghdad; or, as a little girl of eight, having to be polite to a difficult and unkind uncle; or, when she was a beautiful young woman, being imprisoned behind the thick stone walls of the fortress in 'Akká. As long as she was able to bring joy to the heart of Bahá'u'lláh, to stand by the side of 'Abdu'l-Bahá, and to love and support Shoghi Effendi, she was happy. To her, this was the same as being in heaven.

'O thou Maid of Bahá!' wrote Shoghi Effendi. 'Blessed, a thousand times blessed, is he who loves thee . . . and follows in thy footsteps . . .'

Epilogue

Who would have thought that a woman called Sarah who roamed the desert four thousand years ago and never went to school would be remembered today as the mother of nations? Or that an Egyptian queen called Ásíyih would have rescued a Manifestation of God when He was a baby? Or that a girl named Mary who faced disgrace because of a miracle that made her pregnant would be prayed to by millions of people? Or that a little tribal girl called Fátimih would be thought so pure that people now think it would have been wrong even to look at her shadow? Or that a young woman named Táhirih who was only allowed to speak to men from behind a curtain and was martyred because of her belief in new teachings from God would become world famous for proclaiming the equality of men and women? Or that a little Persian girl called Bahíyyih who spent most of her life in poverty, exile or prison would become loved by millions of believers in every part of the world because of her life of service, sacrifice and love?

These six heroines are blessed far beyond our imagination in all the worlds of God.

And we are blessed too when we love them.

O ye handmaids of the merciful Lord!
How many queens of this world laid down their heads
on a pillow of dust and disappeared.
No fruit was left of them, no trace, no sign, not even
their names.
For them, no more granting of bestowals;
for them, no more living at all.
Not so the handmaids who ministered at the Threshold
of God;
these have shone forth like glittering stars
in the skies of ancient glory,
shedding their splendours across all the reaches of time.
'Abdu'l-Bahá

Bibliography

General

'Abdu'l-Bahá. *Selections from the Writings of 'Abdu'l-Bahá*. Haifa: Bahá'í World Centre, 1978.
— *Some Answered Questions*. Wilmette, IL: Bahá'í Publishing Trust, 1981.

The Holy Bible. Authorised King James Version. London: The Gideons, International, 1957.

The Koran [Qur'án]. Trans. J. M. Rodwell. London: Dent (Everyman's Library), 1963.

Lights of Guidance: A Bahá'í Reference File. Compiled by Helen Hornby. New Delhi: Bahá'í Publishing Trust, 5th ed. 1997.

Sarah's Story

'Abdu'l-Bahá. *The Promulgation of Universal Peace*. Wilmette, IL: Bahá'í Publishing Trust, 1982.
— *Some Answered Questions* (ch. 4).

Bahá'u'lláh. *Gleanings from the Writings of Bahá'u'lláh*. Wilmette, IL: Bahá'í Publishing Trust, 1983 (sections 23 and 32).

Bible (Genesis 12–26).

Directives from the Guardian. Compiled by Gertrude Garrida. New Delhi: Bahá'í Publishing Trust, 1973.

Qur'án (surahs 2:119–27; 6:84; 11:72–4; 14:36–42, 50; 22:27; 31:68–70; 37:100–12; 71).

Shoghi Effendi. *The Unfolding Destiny of the British Bahá'í Community: The Messages of the Guardian of the Bahá'í Faith to the Bahá'ís of the British Isles*. London: Bahá'í Publishing Trust, 1981.

Ásíyih's Story

Bible (Exodus 1–24).

Ginzburg, Louis. *Legends of the Jews*, vol. 2. Philadelphia: Jewish Publication Society, 2003.

Qur'án (surahs 7:124; 20:70–5; 28:8–11; 66:11).

The Virgin Mary's Story

Bible (Matthew, Mark, Luke and John; Acts 1:14).

Galvan, Juan. 'Jesus and The Virgin Mary in Islam'. http://www.islamfortoday.com/galvano3.htm

Gaventa, Beverly Roberts. *Mary: Glimpses of the Mother of Jesus*. Edinburgh: T&T Clark, 1999 (this book includes 'The Protevangelium of James', versions of which can also be found online).

Kerr, C. M. 'Joseph, Husband of Mary'. The International Standard Bible Encyclopedia. http://www.searchgodsword.org/enc/isb/view.cgi?number=T5148.

Qur'án (surahs 3, 19 and last verse of 66).

Fátimih's Story

Armstrong, Karen. *Muhammad: A Biography of the Prophet*. London: Phoenix Press, 2004.

Balyuzi, H. M. *Muḥammad and the Course of Islám*. Oxford: George Ronald, 1976.

'Fatimah Bint Muhammad'. http://www.jannah.org/sisters/fatimah.html.

Táhirih's Story

'Abdu'l-Bahá. 'Ṭáhirih', in *Memorials of the Faithful*. Wilmette, IL: Bahá'í Publishing Trust, 1971.

Balyuzi, H. M. *The Báb: The Herald of the Day of Days*. Oxford: George Ronald, 1973.

Johnson, Lowell. *Ṭáhirih*. National Spiritual Assembly of the Bahá'ís of South and West Africa, rev. ed. 1986.

Momen, Moojan. 'The Family and Early Life of Táhirih Qurrat al-'Ayn', in *Baha'i Studies Review*, no. 12, pp. 35–52.

Nabíl-i-A'zam. *The Dawn-Breakers: Nabíl's Narrative of the Early Days of the Bahá'í Revelation*. Wilmette, IL: Bahá'í Publishing Trust, 1970.

Root, Martha L. *Ṭáhirih the Pure*. Los Angeles: Kalimát Press, rev. ed. 1981.

Shoghi Effendi. *God Passes By*. Wilmette, IL: Bahá'í Publishing Trust, rev. ed. 1995.

Taherzadeh, Adib. *The Revelation of Bahá'u'lláh*, vol. 2. Oxford: George Ronald, 1977 (ch. 8).

Bahíyyih Khánum's Story

'Abdu'l-Bahá. *Some Answered Questions* (chs. 11 and 15).

Bahá'u'lláh. *Epistle to the Son of the Wolf.* Wilmette, IL: Bahá'í Publishing Trust, 1988.

Bahíyyih K͟hánum, the Greatest Holy Leaf: A Compilation from Bahá'í Sacred Texts and Writings of the Guardian of the Faith and Bahíyyih K͟hánum's Own Letters. Haifa: Bahá'í World Centre, 1982.

Blomfield, Lady. *The Chosen Highway.* Oxford: George Ronald, rpt. 2007.

Faizi, A.Q. *A Gift of Love Offered to the Greatest Holy Leaf.* Comp. and ed. by Gloria Faizi. 1982.

Khan, Janet A. *Prophet's Daughter: The Life and Legacy of Bahíyyih Khánum, Outstanding Heroine of the Bahá'í Faith.* Wilmette, IL: Bahá'í Publishing Trust, 2005.

Mehrabi, Jacqueline. *Stories of the Greatest Holy Leaf.* London: Bahá'í Publishing Trust, 1997.

'The Passing of Bahíyyih Khánum' and 'The Passing of Bahíyyih Khánum, the Most Exalted Leaf', in *The Bahá'í World, 1932–1934,* vol. 5. rpt. Wilmette, IL: Bahá'í Publishing Trust, 1980 (pp. 22–3; 169–88).

Rabbaní, Rúḥíyyih. *The Priceless Pearl.* London: Bahá'í Publishing Trust, 1969.

Ruhe, David. S. *Door of Hope.* Oxford: George Ronald, 1983.

Notes

Although this book has been written primarily for older children and junior youth, it is hoped that older readers will enjoy it too, and the bibliography and explanatory notes have been added for the interest of anyone wishing to know more about these stories and the reasons for the inclusion or omission of certain material.

1. The quotation at the beginning of the book about the 'immortal heroines' is from Shoghi Effendi, *God Passes By*, p. 347. Other outstanding women from the dispensations of Hinduism, Buddhism and Zoroastrianism are not included here but this does not mean there weren't any. A memorandum dated 23 February 1992 from the Research Department to the Universal House of Justice says 'there have been outstanding women such as Sarah, Ásíyih, the Virgin Mary, Fátimih, Táhirih and the Greatest Holy Leaf in every Dispensation'.

2. You may find that the first three stories (describing the lives of Sarah, Ásíyih and the Virgin Mary) are slightly different from versions you are familiar with. This is because the stories have not just been taken from the Bible but also from the Qur'án, the Bahá'í writings, Jewish legends, Christian accounts not included in the New Testament and the hadíth (sayings of Muhammad which are not in the Qur'án).

3. At times, a choice had to be made as to which version of a name to use. For example, Mary is also known as Maryam in Arabic; and her parents, Anna and Yoachim, are also known as Hannah and Imran; while Abraham is commonly called Ibrahim by Jews and Muslims. All are correct in the culture in which they are used.

4. Moses, Jesus, Muhammad, the Báb and Bahá'u'lláh have a common ancestry that goes back to the family of Abraham, and this is mentioned in biblical, Islamic and Bahá'í writings. For Bahá'u'lláh's lineage see 'Abdu'l-Bahá, *Some Answered Questions*, ch. 57, p. 213; Shoghi Effendi, *God Passes By*, p. 94; and Shoghi Effendi quoted in *Lights of Guidance*, p. 473. For confirmation of a hereditary link between Abraham and Hagar through their son Ishmael to Muhammad, see 'Abdu'l-Bahá, *Some Answered Questions*, ch. 4, p. 13. Five of the 'Immortal Heroines' were also related in some way to Abraham, the exception being Ásíyih.

5. The reason why the biblical account of Abraham's offering to sacrifice His son has been left out of Sarah's story is because the Qur'án states that it was Hagar's son, Ishmael (not Sarah's son, Isaac), who was offered as a sacrifice and this is confirmed in the Bahá'í writings (see Bahá'u'lláh, *Gleanings*, ch. 32, pp. 75–6; Shoghi Effendi, *Unfolding Destiny*, pp. 461–2; and *Directives from the Guardian*, p. 12.)

6. The reference to Abraham being made to walk through fire can be found in several places, including Bahá'u'lláh, *Gleanings*, ch. 23, pp. 56–7, and is associated with the opposition of King Nimrod. Some people may decide to interpret this story literally, as it was a common practice even in the West not so long ago to judge people's innocence or guilt through tests of this kind, or it may be

understood symbolically, as is perhaps suggested in a talk given by 'Abdu'l-Bahá and recorded in the following passage from 'Abdu'l-Bahá, *Promulgation*, p. 399: 'And remember when Nimrod kindled the fire of polytheism whereby he would burn the Friend of God [Abraham]. Verily, we extinguished the fire by the truth and brought upon Nimrod manifest grief.'

7. The building of a shrine or temple by Abraham and Ishmael on a sacred site previously hallowed by Adam is alluded to in the Qur'án, surahs 2:119–21; 3:90–1 and 22:27 and is mentioned in commentaries and traditions of the time. The site is identified as being the one in Mecca called the Ka'bah where Muslims gather for the hajj, or pilgrimage.

8. The differences and similarities between the use of the terms 'Hebrew', 'Israelite' and 'Jew' during the dispensations of Abraham, Moses and Jesus are quite complicated but below is a simplified explanation:

a) See Genesis 10 and 11, and also 14:13, for the biblical source of the word 'Hebrew' and its association with the name of Noah's great, great grandson Heber (or Eber), to whom Abraham was related. One meaning given to 'Hebrew' is 'to pass over' referring to the act of passing over from belief in many gods to belief in one God. Scholars have come up with other possible sources for this name (including it being similar to an ancient Egyptian word meaning 'stranger') but I decided to use the biblical source.

b) The word 'Israelite' came into being after the time of Abraham, when Abraham and Sarah's grandson Jacob was renamed Israel (meaning 'Struggle with God') after an encounter with an angel one night which resulted in Jacob humbly submitting his will to the will of God. The 12 tribes of Israel came from the 12 sons of Jacob/Israel (hence the term 'the children of Israel', who are, in fact, the children of Jacob). The land was divided between the first 11 of them, while the twelfth son, Levi, and his tribe did not own any land but were given the responsible of looking after the temple instead. (This was the tribe Moses' parents came from and also, from some accounts, the ancestral tribe of the Virgin Mary, which links with the stories of her having been educated in the temple in Jerusalem.) When other areas of land were conquered by any of the sons of Israel the inhabitants also became known as Israelites, even though they were not necessarily related by blood directly to Israel.

c) The word 'Jew' is a shortened term which stems from Judah, who was another of Jacob's 12 sons. The tribe of Judah ruled an area of land which became known as Judea. This province is where Jesus came from and it is the reason why He is called a Jew in the Bible (although He was also a Hebrew and an Israelite, as His lineage went back through Jacob (Israel) to Abraham and therefore Heber).

9. A seeming contradiction to the Bible story is Ásíyih's relationship to Pharaoh. The Bible says that it was the Pharaoh's daughter who raised Moses and He was found in the river by her maid, whereas the Qur'án says it was Pharaoh's wife who raised Him and that Moses was found in the river by a palace servant. It is possible that Ásíyih was both wife and daughter, for such marriages did exist at that time, until God revealed through Moses that this practice should cease.

(See 'Abdu'l-Bahá, *Promulgation*, p. 365.) The Qur'án also mentions other details not found in the Bible, including the threat Pharaoh made to those who believed in Moses and what Ásíyih replied. The tale of the gold and hot coals, in which the baby took off Pharaoh's crown, is from a traditional story. Moses' speech impediment is mentioned in Exodus and also in the Bahá'í writings (e.g. see letter written on behalf of Shoghi Effendi in *Unfolding Destiny*, p. 459).

10. Parts of the story about the Virgin Mary have been taken from 'The Protevangelium of James', which is sometimes also called 'the Book of James' and is thought to have been written either in the 1st or 2nd century AD. It is described as being non-canonical and unauthentic by some Church leaders; however, authenticity is given in the Qur'án to some of the incidents it mentions, which is why these have been included here (e.g. Mary giving birth near a date palm and river; surah 19:16–25), which links to the fuller cave account in 'James'; the angel telling Mary's mother that she would have a child although she and her husband were both old; Mary being given into the care of the priest Zacharias; and the casting of lots with rods which resulted in Joseph being chosen to be the husband of Mary (surah 3:35–47). A version of the story of the rods (or arrows) used in the lottery to decide whom Mary should marry has been widely circulated down the centuries, and in 1504 the painter Raphael depicted a scene of Joseph with a rod and dove in his famous work *The Marriage of the Virgin*.

Regarding the approximate date given for the duration of Mary's life (*c.* 15 BC – 50 AD), this has been calculated in relation to the year 1 AD, as that is the commonly accepted date of Jesus' birth, although there is evidence to suggest that He may have been born a few years later.

11. Apart from the historical events relating to Muhammad, which are to be found in several books listed in the bibliography, many of the personal stories about Fátimih were found on Muslim websites. I have only included those most commonly cited and where a reference has been given. They clearly reflect Muhammad's tender love for His daughter and her profound understanding of His station. Regarding the story of the angel Gabriel revealing secret, or hidden, words to Fátimih, this is also mentioned by Shoghi Effendi, who says that the verses entitled the Hidden Words, which Bahá'u'lláh revealed as He paced the banks of the Tigris River, were 'originally designated the "Hidden Book of Fátimih"' and 'identified by its Author with the Book of that same name believed by Shí'ah Islám to be in the possession of the promised Qá'im, and to consist of words of consolation addressed by the angel Gabriel, at God's command, to Fátimih, and dictated to the Imám 'Alí, for the sole purpose of comforting her in her hour of bitter anguish after the death of her illustrious Father' (Shoghi Effendi, *God Passes By*, p. 140). The book was said to have later disappeared, to remain hidden until the Promised One appeared on the Day of Judgement. It was believed that one of the proofs of the Qá'im would be that He would possess it and reveal the hidden, secret meanings of all previous religious texts.

12. Although the story about Bahíyyih Khánum is a few pages longer than the others (her life having taken place more recently and there being more material to draw upon), it is very far from a complete picture of her life. For the purposes of this book it has been kept fairly brief but there is a wealth of other material available (e.g. the carefully researched book *Prophet's Daughter* by Janet Khan; and non-authoritative but nevertheless interesting and inspiring pilgrims' notes that are scattered like gems throughout different publications).

For an insight into her spiritual station, see in particular *Bahíyyih Khánum: The Greatest Holy Leaf*, published by the Baháʼí World Centre, which includes passages from the sacred texts, the writings of the Guardian of the Faith and Bahíyyih Khánum's own letters.

13. There is a sweet link between the past and present on Mount Carmel in the Holy Land. Not far from the grave of Bahíyyih Khánum, and bordering the gardens surrounding the Shrine of the Báb, two steep and narrow streets nestle into the side of the mountain. One is called Shifra and the other Puah. They are named after the two Hebrew midwives who refused to obey the order of Pharaoh to kill all baby boys born to Israelite slaves three thousand years ago.

14. The final quotation, after the Epilogue, is from ʻAbduʼl-Bahá, *Selections,* no. 8, p. 23.